Praise for *Manifesting Something Better*

"I have been privileged to attend Cathy's class on manifestation in the past and found her book on the subject to be the best of the in-person class and more. From basic concepts to different manifestation techniques and possible road blocks to success this book touches on everything you need to know in an easy to understand way. Whether you are new to manifestation or have some experience with it this book will provide you with the tools to take control of the energy you create in your own life."

- Morgan Daimler,
>author of *By Land, Sea, and Sky*
>and *A Child's Eye View of the Fairy Faith*

"The techniques in this book are invaluable. Who said wishes are for children? Catherine shows you how to use positive energy in a way that is simple, direct, as well as very effective. I have used many of these techniques myself with nothing short of wonderful results. So make a wish, simply ask for it. Wouldn't it be wonderful if everyone read this book and learned how to make their life happier, healthier, and just that much more Wonderful?"

-Alexis Doyle
>Internet radio show host
>Cauldron of knowledge
>Liveparanormal.com

"Who doesn't want "what we want (when we want it)"? But how do we attract to ourselves a new job, better weather, a clearer vision, or the many other things that would make our lives better or easier? Catherine Kane leads us gently through the steps of Manifestation. She shows us how it works, how to avoid common ways we neutralize them, and makes it easy to believe that we can do it ourselves. She shares many different techniques, so that each of us can find something that will work for us. She does this all with humor and compassion, her genuine love for her readers coming through the pages, so that, when you are done with the book, you've not only got new skills for a better life, but a new friend."

- Tchipakkan
    Metaphysical speaker and artist
        Host of "The New Normal" on liveparanormal.com
            Co-chair Changing Times, Changing Worlds
                conference

And also for Catherine's previous books

Adventures in Palmistry

"The information in this book is clear, concise, hits the pertinent points of palmistry, and immediately lets you start practicing your craft."

-Adam Latin, professional palmist

"Ms. Kane is not only a talented palm reader, but a talented writer as well. She explains the concepts and techniques clearly, and with a sense of humor."

-Lois Fitzpatrick, leader, East Kingdom Soothsayer's guild, an organization studying the methods and history of psychic readings

The Practical Empath-
Surviving and Thriving as a Psychic Empath

"…Gives you a window of understanding as to who an empath is, a brief synopsis about energy and how it works, shielding techniques, how much input is too much, and so much more. Cathy is an amazing empath who has helped countless people to learn how to deal with this wonderful however sometimes daunting gift. This book makes a great read for the novice and the experienced empath alike. With Cathy's guidance, you will learn how to cope with being an empath and, hopefully, you will get as much, if not more, out of her book *The Practical Empath* as I did. Happy reading."

-Delilah Kieffer, spiritualist and psychic

Manifesting Something Better

Easy, Quick and Fun Ways

To Manifest

The Life of Your Dreams

Also by Catherine Kane

Adventures in Palmistry

The Practical Empath-
Surviving and Thriving as a Psychic Empath

The Lands That Lie Between-
An Urban Fantasy with Morgan and Sam

For more information, please visit Foresight Publications at
www.ForesightYourPsychic.com

Manifesting Something Better

Easy, Quick and Fun Ways
To Manifest the Life of Your Dreams

By Catherine Kane

Foresight Publications
Wallingford, Ct.

Manifesting Something Better ©October2012
by Catherine Kane

All rights reserved.

No part of this book may be reproduced or transmitted in any form, or by any means, electronic or mechanical, including photocopying, recording or by any information storage and retrieval system, without written permission from the author, except for brief quotations in a review.

ISBN 978-0-9846951-1-9

Foresight Publications
Wallingford, CT.

This book is dedicated to
Delilah Kieffer,
one of the most talented
manifestation workers
I've ever known.

Miracles are happening every day,
and you're one of the people
who makes them happen, my friend.

Acknowledgements

As always, I haven't manifested this book alone. I'd like to express my gratitude to the folks who've supported and inspired me in the process of writing this book.

To those of you that I've had the privilege to practice manifestation work with over the years. Whether I've done manifestation on your behalf, worked in partnership with you or taught you how to do it yourself, I've learned from us working together. It's been an honor to be of service.

To Carol, for inspiration to keep going when writing was challenging. Your timely words were the push I needed.

To Jayee White Oak, once again for proofreading, feedback and support with wit, wisdom and lightning speed. You are a wonder to me.

To my readers/reviewers, Alexis, Tchipakkan and Morgan. Your insight and feedback helped make this an even better book. I'm fortunate to have you all in my life.

To the Fairfield County Writer's Group, for continued support and encouragement, live and online. The company of creative spirits feeds my own creativity.

To my readers. You're what keeps me writing, and I hope that we have many more adventures together.

And, as always, to my beloved husband Starwolf, for all of his love, insight and support. You, my love, are one of the best things that the Universe could ever have sent to me.

Table of Contents

How This Book Works 1
Introduction 3
I) The Foundations of Manifestation 5
- 1) What is Manifestation Work? 7
- 2) It's All Energy 13
- 3) What's Your Intention? 21
- 4) Finding Your Focus 27
- 5) The Dragons of Resistance 31
- 6) The Ethics of Manifestation 41
- 7) Choosing a Technique 57
- 8) Making Manifestation a Part of Your Life 63

II) The Processes 69
- A) Preparing Your Energy 71
  - 9) On Preparing Your Energy Field 73
  - 10) The "My Favorite Things" Toolkit 75
  - 11) The "What if Things Got Better?" Technique 83
  - 12) Manifestation at Home 91
  - 13) Share the Wealth 101
- B) Ask 107
  - 14) On Asking 109
  - 15) The "Wouldn't it be nice?" Technique 111
  - 16) Setting an Intention 119
  - 17) The Previewing Technique 125
- C) Receive 131
  - 18) On Receiving 133
  - 19) The "Act as If" Technique 135
  - 20) Paying Attention to Signs from the Universe 141

21) Now, Take Inspired Action 147
D) Multi-purpose 153
22) On Multi-purpose Techniques 155
23) Using Affirmations
(Preparing Your Energy/Asking) 157
24) Working with Gratitude
(Preparing Your Energy/ Receiving) 163

III) Pulling it All Together 169
25) Pulling it All Together 171
26) Don't Stop Now 173

Appendix I) Picking a ManifestationTechnique 175

Glossary 177

How This Book Works

We are always manifesting things in our lives, and manifestation work is a way of getting better control of what we create. This book is designed to help you understand the process of manifestation, and give you tools you need to energetically change your life for the better.

This book is broken into two parts: "The Foundations of Manifestation" and "The Processes". There's also a glossary in the back for easy access to unfamiliar terms.

"The Foundations" is a step by step explanation of manifestation and the basic principles of how it works. Each step builds on the previous one and includes examples of both ways to make it work and things that could cause problems. I'd recommend reading it straight through and in order.

"The Processes" is a collection of different methods and techniques that you can use for the different steps of manifestation. Here you can pick and choose, and read out of order as you wish, according to what seems to be your need at the moment. Eventually, however, I'd recommend that you read and try all of the techniques. The method that's perfect this week may be not so good two weeks later, and knowing your options gives you the best ability to create a life you love.

The above comments are just suggestions, of course. The best way of all to make this book work is to do what works for you. Happy manifesting!

Catherine

Introduction

Have you ever wished upon a star? Bought a raffle ticket and won something? Found that your car breaks down every time you get a little extra money saved up in your bank account?

If so, you've done manifestation. We're all manifesting things all of the time. What we manifest or draw into our lives is largely due to our beliefs and emotions. Beliefs and emotions create the kind of energy that we hold in our bodies and radiate to the universe. What energy we put out into the universe, we tend to get back, whether by manifesting good things or bad. Since that energy shapes the nature of the world around us, it makes sense to learn what we're doing and how to do it so that we get more of the results we want, as opposed to the other kind.

That's what this book is about - how to take control of what you bring into your life, so that you can make your life and the world around you better. While a manifestation technique won't absolutely guarantee you one hundred per cent control over everything that happens in your life, it will help to significantly slant the odds in favor of what you'd want to happen. I don't know about you, but I'm ok with a ninety-nine percent advantage. I'm always glad when the universe is helping me to get where I want to go.

In manifestation work, there are big methods and little ones. This book is about smaller methods that work with less power. We're looking at these smaller methods here because they're simpler to learn, easier to do, fun, and are less likely to trigger our own internal resistance, which means that we don't end up fighting with ourselves. By starting small and simple, you can often actually get where you're going faster and with less trouble, because you'll have fewer self created obstacles to overcome.

We've got a lot of ground to cover, so we'd better get started. Join me in the next section and we'll take a better look at what manifestation work really is.

THE FOUNDATIONS OF MANIFESTATION

Chapter 1
What is Manifestation Work?

Whether you're talking ancient traditions, New Age practices or varied spiritual paths, you'll always find manifestation work in the mix.

What is manifestation work, anyway?

Manifestation work is a general term covering a wide range of ways of working with the energy of the world and the nature of reality around us in order to change things from what they presently are to some other state of being. To put it another way, manifestation work is using non-physical methods to affect and change the physical world.

Some examples of manifestation work in different contexts and cultures are:

- Wishing;
- Spells:
- Invocations;
- Prayers of intercession;
- The Law of Attraction;

And lots of other techniques used to create something new where there was nothing before, or to change the nature of what already exists through working with your word, and your will, and the energy all around you.

We usually think of manifestation work as techniques to create or attract what we desire, but it's worth remembering that manifestation work can also create things that we don't want, when we focus on the wrong kinds of things or when our beliefs make us sabotage ourselves.

Let's take a closer look at how manifestation actually works so we'll know how to create more of the things that we want in our lives and less of the other stuff.

When we talk about manifestation, we need to start with the mind- body connection. In its simplest form, the mind-body connection says that our minds and bodies are connected and affect each other.

People who have heard of the mind-body connection tend to think of it in connection with health and well-being. Some examples of this are that a positive attitude tends to build a stronger immune system, and people who are negative tend to experience pain more severely. That's useful information, but there are other things about the mind - body connection that most people don't know.

The first is that the mind- body connection works in both directions. The mind not only affects the body – the body can also affect the mind. For instance, choosing more positive body language (more upright posture, your shoulders back and relaxed, good eye contact) can decrease timidity and increase feelings of confidence.

The second (and the one that applies more to manifestation) is that the mind-body connection doesn't only affect your mind and body. It can actually change the nature of reality and the world around you.

Everything, including you and me, is made up of energy and every person is surrounded by an energy field. The kind of energy in our energy field tends to shape the world around us through attraction and manifestation. The nature of that energy is determined largely by our emotions, thoughts and beliefs, through the mind-body connection.

We'll be getting into this in more detail in the chapter on energy. For now, just keep in mind that our emotions, thoughts and beliefs determine our energy and our energy field is a key part of manifestation work.

Most conscious, or intentional, manifestation work is meant to change things for the better - into something the person working considers preferable or desirable. It makes good things happen. Unfortunately, our unconscious beliefs can make us manifest desirable or undesirable things, based on what kind of energy and beliefs we have.

We're all manifesting all of the time, and what we attract is based on our energy, beliefs and focus. If we keep these positive, we tend to manifest more of what we want. If we give most of our time and attention to focusing on negative things, we can actually manifest things we don't want with the same power we can use to manifest positive ones.

We'll be looking at this point as well in the chapter on energy. For now, the key thing is that you can manifest negative things as well as positive ones, and what you create is largely based on what you believe and what you focus on.

Another factor to look at in an overview of manifestation is the question of manifestation itself. When we do the work, do we really create something out of nothing to have what we're looking for, or does something else happen?

It depends.

The Universe can do pretty much anything. It's generous, magical and amazing – but it also knows that the shortest distance between two points is a straight line. For this reason, it will often use the method that's easiest, most appropriate and most energetically economical to bring what you're trying to call into your life. Sometimes this means manifesting something out of nothing. Sometimes this means arranging things so that it's attracted into your life.

It's like being homebound and running out of cookies. You can call a friend to bring you more cookies, in effect attracting them into your life, or you can get out the ingredients and bake some, manifesting them where there were no cookies before. (You can also throw on a coat and go get your own cookies, but that's a non-energetic, although legitimate, approach.) It's good to know that there are different ways of bringing cookies to you, but the end result is that, either way, you've got cookies.

Just as with the cookies, when you do manifestation work, it may result in you manifesting something or in attracting it to you. The difference is important and it isn't, because the end result in either case is your area of the cosmos being altered to include what you wanted and asked for.

And that's what counts the most.

There are lots of ways to manifest what you want in life. There are powerful techniques and gentle ones, quick ones and ones that take time, structured ones and flexible ones, blatant ones and subtle ones. They all have their individual strengths and weaknesses, but there are certain elements they all seem to hold in common.

When I look closely at the foundation of all manifestation work, it breaks down to one basic formula:

- Energy
  plus
- Intention (the goal you have set)
  plus
- Focus (your technique or method)
  equals
- Manifestation

Any manifestation work is a lot like a laser beam. You tap into the energy of the world around you, chose your target by setting an intention, and focus and concentrate that energy through the lens of the manifestation technique, in order to achieve your purpose.

We'll be looking at these individual steps in more detail first, and then how to combine them in different manifestation techniques. Keep the basic formula in mind as you read, and the whole process will make a lot more sense.

Energy + Intention + Focus= Manifestation.

The rest all lies in the details.

To summarize this overview of manifestation work:

- Manifestation work is seen in one form or other in most spiritual or metaphysical cultures.
- Our energy can shape the nature of the world around us.
- Our thoughts and beliefs determine what kind of energy we have in our energy fields.
- We are always manifesting, whether we know it or not.
- We can manifest good things and bad things.
- Manifestation work can happen through literal creation of something out of nothing, or through attracting the people, things, situations and opportunities into our lives.
- Most manifestation techniques seem to work by combining energy, an intention, and a manifestation work technique to manifest a particular goal.

Whew! That's a fair amount of information, and we're only just at the beginning. Let's move on now to the next chapter on energy, the foundation of manifestation.

Chapter 2
It's All Energy

One thing I use manifestation work for is parking spots.
One busy weekend, my husband and I were doing errands, and it was only when we turned down the parking lot aisle that I realized I hadn't set a parking intention yet.
As he drove, I hastily started to set an intention for a parking spot close to the door we would use.
Before I even finished, a car pulled out of the third spot from the entrance...
I looked at Starwolf. He looked at me.
"That's impressive, even for you" he said as he pulled into the spot.

The process of manifestation begins with energy - the energy inside of you, in your energy field, in the world around you. Everything is made up of energy, and the way that different energies interact can create or destroy things.

In Western mind, we historically think of things as solid. A tree, a table, your hand - these are all solid things you can see and touch and are therefore immutable. Eastern mind, on the other hand, historically sees everything as being made of energy, whether called "chi", "ki" or by some other name, and works with the world accordingly. (For examples, look at practices like accupressure or tai chi.)

Interestingly enough, as Western science has progressed, we've made discoveries that bring us closer to the Eastern way of seeing things. We've found, for instance, that a tree or table or hand that seems so solid is actually made up of atoms, and that atoms are tiny particles with a great deal of space between them, held together by energetic attraction, both nuclear and magnetic. Solids are mostly large areas of space filled with energy, and the impression of solidity is somewhat of an illusion.

Energy doesn't just stay where it's put, either. We've all heard how the magnetic fields of stars and planets interact and affect each other. Like them, the energetic fields of things in this world can also have an effect on other things around them, and this includes the energy that people are made of.

Everything is made out of energy. It all starts there.

When we look at magnetic energy and how it works, magnets have two poles- a positive and a negative one. When we look at personal energy, we think of positive and negative energy as well, but instead of being one or the other, personal energy tends to fall more along a range, with very positive at one end, and very negative at the other.

Positive energy tends to be more uplifting and creative. It supports better health in body, mind and spirit, success, and makes manifesting the positive things we want easier for us.

Negative energy, on the other hand, tends to be more draining and destructive. It can sabotage your life, kill your dreams and damage your health. It also makes it much harder to manifest the things you would like (although it does make it far easier to attract the things that you don't want.)

The more positive you are, the easier it is to

manifest the things you want. It's not always easy but there are a lot of good reasons to try to keep your energy as positive as possible.

The next thing to look at is the concept of attraction. Energy fields are magnetic and tend to attract or repel each other, and that power of attraction is part of how manifestation work happens.

In the study of energy, like calls to like. Energy tends to attract more energy that is similar to it and knowing that is an important principle that makes it easier to manifest things.

Have you ever been to one of those parties where a whole bunch of different kinds of people are invited? The sports types will tend to gather in one area and the business mavens in another and the artistic folks in a third.

It's like that party. Like calls to like. This means that, when you're trying to manifest something, it's easiest to attract something that's like the energy in your own energy field. If you're cultivating a major grudge and are trying to manifest sunshine and daisies, you'll have an uphill climb of it, whereas if you can put your energy in a more positive state, you'll find the process much simpler.

It also means that, when you're trying to manifest something, you'll not only be more likely to succeed if your goal matches your own energy, but you'll also have the tendency to attract other things that have a similar energy to your original goal. For instance, say I have an important letter with good news on the way and I'm working to help it arrive today. If my energy's positive, my letter may not only show up but I may also get a positive phone call or "just happen to" stumble across a new book by a favorite author.

Like calls to like. It's far easier to manifest the positive things we want if we start with a positive energy field.

The next question is, since it attracts more good things and helps us to manifest things we want more easily, how do we make our energy fields more positive? As I mentioned in the last chapter, the vibrational level of our energy fields tends to be set by the emotions we feel, the thoughts we think, the beliefs we hold, and the stories that we tell ourselves.

Tell yourself you're born to win? Things will probably come easier for you. Tell yourself that bad things always happen to you? You'll also tend to find that happens. It's that principle of "Like calls to like" at work in your life – and it manifests negative things as well as positive ones, dependant on what beliefs and situations you give most of your attention to. The interesting thing about that is that, when folks can let go of negative beliefs and start to have more positive ones, what happens in their lives also tends to improve. This is one reason that a positive attitude is important. It sets the level on your energy field, which determines what you're manifesting at any point.

A lot of your emotions and attitude come from your beliefs, conscious and unconscious. We all have beliefs that help us, but we also have ones that limit or even hurt us lurking around in our unconscious minds. Many of these are beliefs that served us in the past but are no longer helpful, or beliefs taught to us by people who were mistakenly thinking that they were protecting or otherwise helping us.

It's a good idea to every now and again do some mental housecleaning and examine our beliefs, in order to determine whether they're still true for us and what they may be drawing into our lives. Beliefs are like t-shirts. If they no longer fit us, they should be pulled out of our mental chest of drawers and put in the box for recycling.

It's important to be aware of your energy. It's important to pay attention to the thoughts you're thinking, the things you're focusing on, the feelings you're holding onto and the stories you're telling yourself because they affect that energy; and it's important to be as positive as you can in any given moment.

Personal energy is not strictly positive or negative. It lays along that range from very positive to very negative, and most of us shuttle back and forth within this energetic scale; but the more positive that we can be at any moment, the easier it is to manifest positive things.

Don't get me wrong here. There's nobody who's 100% positive all of the time. We all have bad hair days, and most of us have been down or depressed at some time in our lives.

The good news is that is that it's not an "all-or-nothing" proposition. You don't have to be perfect to have energy good enough to make good things happen.

- For temporary bad moods, there is usually a bit of lead time before the attitude starts to affect your energy field. This is usually enough time to notice what's happening and choose a better thought.
- For challenging times and conditions like chronic depression, even then you have options. You don't have to be perfect. There are ways to lift your spirits and improve your feelings and even a small upturn in your emotions can improve your energy and start attracting better things to you than you were experiencing previously (This can help you to shift your emotions and energy upwards even further.)

The challenge is therefore not perfection. It is to always have the most positive thoughts and therefore the most positive energy that you're capable of at any individual moment, so that you attract the most positive experiences possible at that time and so that it's as easy as possible to manifest what you want.

The good thing is that we don't have to be perfect. We don't have to be perfectly positive to manifest good things in our lives, but the more positive we can keep our energy at any particular moment, the more good things we automatically attract and the easier it is to consciously manifest the things that we want in our lives.

The best that we can do is the best that we can do, and thankfully that seems to be good enough.

Everything is made of energy, and it all starts there. By being aware of our energy and keeping it as positive as possible, we attract better things and make it easier to manifest the things that we want.

We'll be talking in later chapters about some specific methods you can use to improve the level of your energetic field. For now, remember that the more positive your emotions, thoughts and beliefs are, the more positive your energy will be and the more positive things you will attract into your life.

Next, let's move on to where that energy is going. Let's look at goals and intentions.

Chapter 3
What's Your Intention?

When doing manifestation work, you start first with energy, and then decide what you want to do with that it. You set an intention of what you want to accomplish.

What is "setting an intention"? An "intention" is just a "fancy-schmancy" term in metaphysics for a goal that you are "intending" to achieve. "Setting an intention" is the term for choosing such a goal and locking on to it. Once you have your intention solidly in mind, it will be the target you focus on while working with energy to manifest things.

A good intention is essential to manifesting what you want, and there are two main things to think about in the process of setting the best intention possible – knowing what you want and how specific to be. Let's look at both.

When setting an intention, the first thing to be sure of is to know what you really want.

That doesn't sound very hard, but people have more problems with this step than with most of the others. You see, friends and family and society and the media are all very big on telling us what we should want in order to be happy/sexy/ healthy/successful in life. Lots of times we get off track on our own dreams because we listen too much to everyone else.

The truth is that we don't all really want or need the same things...

When climbing the ladder of success, it's important to make sure that you've leaned it against the right wall.

Many people spend their lives chasing other folks' dreams because they've let people convince them that this is what they really want themselves. The fast car, the expensive house with the ritzy address, the status job or the trophy wife. They find out later in life that these particular things don't bring them happiness at all, and then they have to start all over. Many never find their happiness in this lifetime because of all the time they wasted chasing the wrong dreams.

In manifestation work, just as in life, you want to be clear on what you really want, so you don't end up heading in the wrong direction. While the supply of energy in the Universe is for all practical purposes infinite, your time's not quite as unlimited, so it's better to choose the right intention, rather than have to go back and do it twice.

How do you figure out what you really want? There are two things to consider here:

- Sorting out what you want from what everyone else wants,
- And figuring out why you want it.

We've already said that not everyone wants the same thing, and that it's important go after what **you** want, as opposed to things people say you **should** want. It's also important to know that many times we're not pursuing a particular item or experience as much as we're chasing the beliefs or feelings we have about it.

That's why two people can want the same thing for

different reasons.

- One person can want a college degree because, to him, it symbolizes competence and achievement; the other because it means increased income and status.
- One can want to be rich because she feels that it'll make her feel safe; the other because she believes that it will give her freedom to do what she loves.

In truth, these people don't really want the degree or money as much as they want the feelings of competence, status, security or freedom.

Fortunately, there's a magic word that you can use both to sort out what you want from what people say you should want <u>and</u> also to help find the desired emotion behind the thing or experience.

The magic word is "Why?" To get to the heart of what you really want, keep asking yourself "Why do I want that?"

- I want a trip around the world.
- "Why do I want that?"
- Because it'll be fun.
- "Why do I want that?"
- Because I feel tense now with everything I'm doing, and I want to feel more relaxed
- "Why do I want that?"
- Because it feels good
- "Why do I want that?"

Keep going until no more answers surface. Often the answer you'll get to at last is "Because it feels good to…" or something like that. That's the point where you've gotten to the heart of it and what you really want, as opposed to what people tell you that you want.

The person in this example might enjoy a trip, but what he really wants most is to relax and feel good. That's what his intention should be, not a trip per se. Maybe this intention will manifest as a trip; maybe as a free day at the spa; maybe his nasty boss will move away; and maybe he'll win a million dollars and be free to relax in any way he sees fit.

Use the power of "why" to cut through illusions and find out what you really want in to set the best intention possible. You'll get the best results when you ask for what you really want.

The second question in setting an intention is how specific should you be?

Some sources believe you should be as specific as possible, to be sure that you get exactly what you want, down to the last iota. Other sources believe you should leave it wide open so the Universe can give you whatever is the best option for you.

I'm afraid I fall smack in the middle of this. I believe you should be as specific as you need to be **and no more so.** My experience has been that, even when I'm sure that I know what I want, the Universe often comes up with even more excellent things I hadn't thought of. The Universe frequently meets my needs in more creative and much better ways that I'd planned, if I leave room in my intention for this to happen. If I leave the Universe "wiggle room", it loves to surprise and delight me, and so I've learned to leave that wiggle room.

For you, that means that if what you want is a car, ask for a car. If there's a reason it's important that it's red, ask for a red car. However, if what you really want is reliable transportation, ask for "reliable transportation".

The Universe might send you a car; or it might send you a van, or even a wealthy lover who drives you everywhere you want, whenever you want. By being as specific as you need and no more so, you leave room for even better things than you'd thought of. That can not only be better for you, but great fun besides.

We'll be talking later on in this book about using setting an intention for asking for what you want in the section "Ask" in the processes. For now, just keep in mind that, to get someplace, you need to first decide where you're going. Setting an intention is how you do that.

We know what we want. We get to the feelings behind the things we're manifesting. We're as specific as we need, and no more so. We set the intention we will be sending energy to.

And we prepare to do the manifestation work.

In the next chapter, let's talk about how to focus that energy on that intention.

Chapter 4
Finding Your Focus

We've looked at energy. We've set a goal or intention. The next step is to focus that energy on that intention so it can start to work to bring the situation or thing we want into our lives. That's where the techniques in this book come in. They're tools that you use to work with energy and focus it on your intention.

Each method has its' own strengths and individual aspects, but there are things that all methods of focusing energy have in common. We'll be looking at those here.

Let's start with the basics.

What you focus on most is what you tend to draw more of into your life. If you're counting your blessings, you tend to draw more blessings. If, on the other hand, you're focusing more on what's wrong with your life.... well, you get the idea.

When you give your time, your attention, your focus, your love, your resources to something, it tends to increase in your life - not just because you're spending more time on it, but also because having your attention there is part of what sets the vibration on your energy field and affects what that field attracts to it.

Furthermore, if you're focusing on one thing, you won't only tend to attract more of that particular thing. You'll also tend to attract other things that also vibrate at the same energetic level or feel the same way. For instance, if you're focusing on manifesting chances to sell your crafts in stores, you may not only find more of those chances popping up. You may also start getting offers to showcase your creations online or on a TV broadcast. (You may also find more hot fudge sundaes just "popping up" because these are all "happy things.")

This is why it's easier to manifest positive things if your energy is already positive. You're already on the right frequency, and your energy lends its strength to attract things that match that positive energy.

As you remember, like calls to like. Any technique is just a way of putting your focus on your intention and keeping it there so you manifest things that you want as opposed to random things from the world around you. When you focus your attention on things you want, you're sending a message to the Universe saying "Send me more of this, please."

And the Universe complies...

Once you've got your intention set and your energy on board, the way most techniques work is by focusing your will on what you want. In the physical world, this would be motivation and persistence – to get what you want you have to stick with it and find the strength and desire to do the work to make things change. In the metaphysical world, it's like that, except you're doing the heavy lifting with your spirit as opposed to your knees.

Your will is at the heart of everything you do in life, both on the physical and metaphysical planes. Things happen when you decide that they will happen, they **must** happen, and with that decision, put your energy and your actions behind your intention or goal.

Strictly speaking, you could do manifestation work purely by focus of will alone, but using the techniques in this book will help you focus your will and bring that energy to bear upon the manifestation.

One of the key points of manifestation work is developing the belief that things are going to happen, or, failing that, at least that things <u>could</u> happen. There are a number of different ways to experience this.

- The calm surety that things are on the move.
- The firm, strong feeling that things are going to happen because you will make them happen.
- The magical "Christmas morning" feeling of anticipation, where you're not sure of exactly what's going to happen, but you know it's going to be great.

Or any other feelings that support the manifestation.

I have a bumper sticker that says "Something Wonderful is About to Happen." I know that I am on my way when I start to feel that calm, centered, happy feeling that matches the energy of that bumper sticker.

By believing in the possibility of an energetic change, you strengthen your focus and the manifestation work itself.

The basic steps of manifestation:

- You prepare your energy and keep it as positive as possible.
- You set an intention. You pick a goal.
- You ask for what you want. You focus that energy on your intention with your will by using a manifestation technique.
- And finally, you prepare to receive what you have asked for.

Pretty straight forward, right? But before we're ready to start working with manifestation techniques, we still need to look at one more thing. Let's visit the dragons of resistance, see how we block our own prosperity and learn how to stop doing that.

Chapter 5
The Dragons of Resistance

There are lots of different ways of working with energy and focus to manifest a different reality around you. Some of these techniques are stronger and more powerful, while some are less so. At that point, why wouldn't you always want to use the biggest, baddest, most powerful method that you could lay your hands on?

Sometimes you will, but it's not always in your best interests to do so. Depending on what you're trying to change, a frontal assault on your current reality can trigger your own inner resistance. If this happens, you have to overcome your world's tendency to stay as it is, <u>and</u> your own inner fears and beliefs, and those makes the job of transformation even tougher.

As you know, our energy is created in part from our beliefs, both our conscious and unconscious. The hard part about this is that the energy comes out of negative beliefs as well as positive ones; and boy, do we have an awful lot of limiting and negative beliefs lurking in our conscious and unconscious minds. Those negative or limiting beliefs generate resistance.

Resistance is usually a belief mechanism of your unconscious mind. It happens when there's too extreme a gap between what we currently believe, and the changes we are trying to make. When the difference is too great between the two concepts (and how much is too much will vary), our unconscious mind thinks we're going into something unsafe and starts sending out negative signals that can sabotage what we're trying to accomplish. It's just trying to protect us, but it can still cause some major problems.

For instance, say you've been overweight for awhile and you decide to shed those extra pounds. Unconsciously, you see yourself as that heavier person, and your mind tends to hang on to that as what's real. Besides that, you've probably got some unconscious beliefs in conflict with losing weight ("Being on a diet means giving up eating things that I like.", "Losing weight is hard work.", "Thin people are mean.", and "The core word in "diet" is "die." are a few that leap to mind.) At that point, because you have negative beliefs about losing weight and your unconscious favors the reality it knows, resistance rears its ugly head and you not only have to fight your metabolism, but your mind-body connection as well.

Your unconscious mind goes to work. If you're using affirmations ("I lose weight quickly and easily"), your unconscious starts making sardonic and cynical little comments. ("Yeah, right. You'll always be built like a hippo.") You'll find yourself with urges to cheat on your diet "just a little bit". People bearing cheesecakes will "just turn up" in your area. You'll hurt yourself or the car won't start, so you can't go to the gym and exercise.

And eventually, you'll give up trying (often when you're at least five pounds heavier).

Now, given that your mind can help you do such amazing things, why would it go and shoot you in the foot like this? It's because, when you're trying to make a significant change in your reality (whether the physical discipline of losing ten more pounds or the energetic manifestation of the loving partner of your dreams), your unconscious tends to throw its weight behind reality as you currently understand it to be, until you can change those beliefs (or at least loosen them up) enough to get your unconscious to support that new reality. The unconscious mind sees that extreme goal as impossible, based on beliefs it currently holds. It'll try to stop us from going there in order to keep us "safe" in the reality we currently live in. According to your current beliefs, the reality you know feels "safer" because you know how it works, even if you don't like it; and change feels "unsafe" and "scary."

It's like physics. "A body in motion remains in motion and a body at rest remains at rest until acted on by an irresistible force." Most people's realities prefer to remain stable in a situation they're already familiar with. It takes effort and energy (that irresistible force) to get them to begin to move and shift over to something new.

You don't necessarily want to use every possible bit of force you can manage, though. In manifestation, too much power is often as bad as too little for actually triggering a reality shift in a smooth and easy fashion. Too little force is not enough to make reality shift to where you want it. Too much force can trigger resistance, making change even more difficult, so you need more effort just to get anywhere at all.

The bottom line is to use as much energy as you need to get things in motion - and no more so. This helps avoid triggering inner resistance, and making your struggle more difficult than it needs to be.

Different people experience resistance in different ways. There are symptoms that let you know when you're experiencing resistance, and these come in four basic flavors:

- Physical symptoms of resistance.
- Mental symptoms of resistance.
- Emotional symptoms of resistance.
- Situational symptoms of resistance (otherwise known as "co-incidences.")

Physical symptoms of resistance often duplicate the physical reactions of stress, anxiety or fear. You may feel muscle tension in your neck or back or jaw. You may feel sick to your stomach. You may feel the hairs rise on the back of your neck or suddenly feel hyper-alert, and anticipating trouble.

Mental symptoms of resistance tend to build obstacles to moving in a direction. You'll come up with really good reasons why you should do that thing later or better yet, not at all. You may find yourself distractible, mentally "wandering off" or "getting fuzzy". You may find yourself excessively focused on something else altogether.

Emotional symptoms show up as negative emotions. You may feel stressed, anxious, afraid, or angry. You may link these emotions to the topic generating the resistance, or you may not realize where they're coming from, ending up with free floating fear or anxiety, or undirected anger.

Finally, if your resistance is strong enough, you may actually start manifesting things to protect you from manifesting things. (Ironic, that!) You may get sick. Your car may break down. You may have unexpected expenses, mandatory overtime or other demands on your time that get in the way of you moving in the direction of what you're trying to manifest. Unless you figure out what's going on, you may think these are just unfortunate "co-incidences."

Now, this isn't saying every tense jaw, or bit of anxiety, or schedule gone awry means resistance, but these symptoms can let us know when we're experiencing it. Fortunately, there are a couple of ways that we can figure this out.

First, we can figure out our own personal symptoms of resistance in advance, so when they happen in response to a situation, we're aware of what's happening.

Try this. First, think of something you really don't like or are afraid of, such as snakes, taxes or dental surgery. Close your eyes and picture the situation using sights sounds and as many other senses as possible.

Stop and pay attention. How does your body feel? What emotions are you feeling? What are your thoughts doing?

Now, change over to thinking about something you really like, such as chocolate, a favorite place, or someone you love.

Stop and pay attention again. What has changed? How does your body feel now? How are your emotions different? What kind of thoughts are you thinking?

Those different experiences in the first part tell you a lot about how resistance will feel to you, and changing your focus helps to make them clearer and more obvious.

As for situational or "co-incidence" symptoms, the easiest way to identify them is to look over our own histories and watch for patterns that repeatedly block us from reaching our dreams.

As one example, there was a point earlier in my life when I wasn't comfortable having a lot of money. Every time my bank account went over $500, my car would break down and the repairs would bring me back down into that "comfort" range again. It wasn't until years later that I finally realized what I was doing to myself and how powerful my unconscious manifestation was then.

If you find the same pattern or "co-incidence" cropping up every time you're moving out of your comfort zone towards something you want but are not familiar with, this may be resistance raising up its dragon head.

Once you're familiar with the signs and symptoms of how resistance acts in your life, you can watch for those signs and use them to slow down or power forward, whichever is most appropriate.

When I think about resistance, I tend to think about those climactic scenes in fantasy novels where the hero must go into a cave and steal something from the dragon's horde without bringing the dragon down upon himself and his companions.

If the hero marches in shouting challenges, kicks the dragon in the snout and then brandishes his vorpal sword flamboyantly in the direction of the dragon's left eye, he usually quickly becomes dragon chow. On the other hand, if he muffles his armor so it won't jingle or clash and his shoes so they won't clomp; if he moves quietly and carefully as he enters into the dragon's lair; if he freezes when the dragon stirs in his sleep until the monstrous wyrm turns over and goes deeper into slumber; the odds increase dramatically that he'll emerge alive and unharmed, as well as with his objective.

That's why you might not always want to use the most powerful techniques for manifestation work available. Some times "More power!" is the theme song of the day, but often charging head on at the problem with all the "oomph!" you can muster only wakes up the dragons of resistance, leaving you metaphorically flambéed and worse off than you were before. Sometimes, "less" really is "more." At that point, using a less powerful but more subtle technique may avoid triggering the dragons at all, making the challenge of change or manifestation much easier and quicker for you than fighting your way uphill against the resistance you've piled up through all of your life.

Sometimes, if the dragons of resistance stir and open one eye as you try to sneak by them, a less powerful technique makes them think "No real threat there...", roll over and go back to sleep as you tip toe by them and achieve your goal in an effortless manner.

Do you see what I'm getting at here? Big technique plus big resistance equals big challenge to overcome. Small technique versus no resistance can actually result in a smaller obstacle to face and an easier change of reality.

That's why you might actually do better to choose a small or less powerful technique, rather than bring up the big guns right away.

It's good to keep resistance in mind when you're planning on doing manifestation work, and chose the methods that will make things happen for you without awakening the Dragons of Resistance.

Lower power manifestation techniques are good for avoiding resistance, but sometimes, no matter how careful we are or how gentle the techniques, we can't avoid encountering it if we want to accomplish anything at all.

As noted earlier, a body at rest remains at rest until acted on by that irresistible force. Change in our lives acts like that as well. There are many times that, if we find the way to apply leverage at the right angle, we can subtly slide our resting lives gradually into motion without encountering any resistance. There are also many times when we're so firmly entrenched in current reality that we've dug ourselves into a metaphorical rut. At that point, there will probably be some degree of resistance or other before we can get ourselves out of that hole and on the move once more.

The question then is "Can you get by without resistance or do you have to work through it?"

Sometimes we can't avoid resistance. At that point, the objective can be to minimize it. Maybe we need to slow down on the technique we're using to decrease or eliminate the resistance. Maybe we need to try a different technique. Maybe we need to revise our intention to a smaller one. (Remember how resistance is triggered by too big a perceived gap between what you're going for and what you have now?) This doesn't mean that you'll never get your original intention, but rather that reaching it by using an intermediate step may wash away resistance and make the process move faster.

Sometimes, no matter what you do, you can't avoid

resistance. At that point, you may want to look at your intention and make sure that you're going in the right direction. (Resistance is sometimes a cue that we're turned around.) If you are, then do what you can to minimize resistance and settle in for a more prolonged and challenging process. This is the kind of situation where the more powerful techniques not covered in this book can be useful, but many times by avoiding resistance, you don't need that much power.

In all of these cases, choosing the best method for your current task will make that transformation as simple as it is possible to be. If we can avoid or minimize resistance, we generally make our challenge easier. A low power technique may not always seem the optimal choice at first, but if we choose the lowest power method that's still effective, we can minimize or avoid resistance.

To sum things up, resistance is important to keep in mind when doing manifestation work. Resistance comes out of our thoughts and beliefs and our unconscious mind's attempts to keep us "safe" by keeping us in a reality we already know. It can be overcome if you're willing to put enough "muscle" into the process, but many times, the best choice is to use a less powerful technique that moves us towards our goal slightly more slowly, but avoids resistance.

By avoiding resistance, we make the trip to our new reality simpler and easier, and this can make energetic change much easier for us.

Chapter 6
The Ethics of Manifestation

When you talk manifestation work, one question is why should you worry about ethics? If anything's possible and these energywork techniques can open the cosmos to us, why put any limits, ethical or otherwise, on ourselves? Why not just run amok?

Well, there are good reasons for paying attention to ethics in manifestation work, as in any type of metaphysics. These include:

- When you do good things, your energy becomes more positive, and positive energy attracts positive experiences.
- When you act in harmony with your beliefs, you can shape the kind of person you are and who you become. When you do things you believe are right, your energy's more positive and you feel good about yourself. This makes you feel more worthy of good things and decreases blocks to manifestation.
- When you do things you feel are sneaky or wrong, you tend to feel bad about yourself. That generates negative energy, which tends to attract negative experiences.

In short, being ethical makes it easier to manifest good things, and being unethical tends to attract the bad ones. Ethics are the right thing to do, but they also improve the overall quality of your life from an energetic standpoint. This is why it's important to understand ethics and act ethically in manifestation. When you're doing the right things, manifestation tends to be easier and quicker, with less resistance to struggle against. Let's look at the ethics of manifestation, and how your beliefs affect energy work.

In this world, some people believe that benefitting from your own metaphysical work is unethical, and leads to misfortune. They have problems with the idea of using energywork or magick for their own benefit at all. Other people believe you can do energywork on your own behalf as long as you do it ethically.

As we know, our beliefs shape the nature of the world around us and attract people, things and experiences that support those beliefs. This means that, whether you believe it's ethical to do manifestation work for yourself or not, you're right because you'll tend to manifest a world where those beliefs are accurate. At that point, it's important to consider your beliefs about what's ethical – whether they really reflect how you feel about the world, and whether they support what is good for you and others in that world. Sometimes we accidentally pick up unconscious beliefs that don't help us, so it's important to pay attention.

From where I sit, I feel that, if it's ethically appropriate for me to do something in the physical world, it's also ethical to do it energetically. In the physical world, I can take action to help myself and improve my own situation, as long as I don't try to do it at the expense of someone else, and I believe it's the same thing in manifestation work.

You may believe this or you may not. You're definitely entitled to believe what you choose on this. I would just encourage you to pay attention to what you believe and be sure that your unconscious and conscious beliefs are in harmony with each other, so you're not working against yourself.

Let's look at some of the ethical questions around manifestation work, and how we can approach these issues for the highest good of all concerned.

Let's start with the most common ethical issue– the belief that all energywork or magick is spiritual, and that it's wrong to use spiritual gifts to materially benefit.

People who believe this tend to believe that spiritual things are spiritual and material things are material, and never the twain shall meet. They believe that using your spiritual gifts to do something for yourself such as make money, find a life partner or get a job somehow taints or cheapens the spiritual gift and may even cause you to lose that ability.

You can choose to believe this, but it hasn't been my experience. I find that the world is full of many different things, and they're all interconnected. This includes the spiritual and the material. As an example, you can fast and focus on meditation to emphasize the spiritual and be less concerned with the material world. That can work in moderation, but if you carry it too far, excessive fasting can make your body weak or sick, interfering with your ability to focus and meditate.

To do your best in the spiritual world, you need to nurture yourself in the material world. To do your best in the material world, you need to keep in connection with the spiritual world. They're interconnected and we need both parts of our being. At that point, we can't "cheapen" or diminish our more spiritual gifts if we use them in an ethical fashion to support us in more material concerns, because it all works together.

Related to the previous issue is the idea that manifestation work is a gift from spirit and it's wrong to benefit personally from the use of your spiritual skills. There are some people who see all varieties of magick and manifestation as Spirit working through them or as a gift from Spirit; as opposed to a skill they have been given. Believing that the ability belongs to Spirit, as opposed to being their own, they feel it's wrong to take credit for any positive things they do with that gift. They also tend to believe that it's wrong to charge for or indeed receive any recompense at all for using that gift.

You're welcome to believe that if you like but that's something else that has not been my experience in life. I'd agree that the ability to work with energy for manifestation is a gift from Spirit - but I also feel that such things as athletic prowess, an ability to make connections with people, and a knack for figures are also gifts from the Spirit, and no one sees anything wrong with people using those gifts on their own behalf. No one is dismayed by the natural athlete making money in sports, the people person attracting a life partner or the numbers cruncher becoming an expert accountant, so there seems no reason why the energy worker should be penalized for or forbidden from benefitting from his own gift as long as he does it ethically.

When you give someone a gift, you expect them to open it up and use it themselves.

I believe that spiritual gifts are like any other gifts from Spirit; and they're fine to use to help yourself as long as you do it ethically.

Another group of beliefs that blocks people from doing manifestation for themselves is a category called "scarcity beliefs". These are various beliefs that say there's only so much good stuff to go around, so, if you manifest something good for yourself, it's taken away from someone else. In more simple terms, people with scarcity beliefs believe that, for someone to win, someone else must lose…

Now it is true that if you're vying for a specific item, such as a particular job or specific partner in love, if one person gets it, another one doesn't., but there are ethical ways of manifesting good things for yourself without harming others.

First, using a job as an example, you can work to manifest the "job that you are best suited for and that is best suited for you." This means that if you belong in a particular job, you'll get it, and if not, the energywork will sweep you along to something else that's a better fit for you.

Second, remember that not everyone wants the same thing. In cars, some like sports cars and some like cargo haulers. In dates, some folks like blondes and some prefer brunettes. This means that there's not as much of a shortage as you might think because we're not all competing for the same things.

Last, it's possible for us all to win as long as we ask responsibly. We can't all marry the same person, but all of us who wish to marry have the potential to find a partner who's a good match. We can't all simultaneously be President of the United States, but we can all have meaningful jobs that support us.

There is enough in the world for everyone to be happy.

Yet another reason that people worry about doing manifestation work is that "it's just not fair."

"It's just not fair to use energywork to get the edge over someone else."

"It's an unfair advantage."

"It's taking advantage of people."

They feel working with energy is a special gift that not everyone has, and if they use these skills, they're cheating or having an unfair edge over the people around them somehow.

This is not accurate for a couple of reasons.

First, if you want to change your life, no one will consider it unfair if you:

- Set goals and make plans for how you're going to accomplish this;
- Learn new skills to achieve that change;
- Give up old habits to dedicate more time to moving towards your dreams;
- Do the work to change your life;
- Save money to pay for something;

- Go back to school;
- Commit to exercising or study or other practices that create the new you;

Or do any of a million other things that people do every day when they want to get stronger, wiser, healthier; find a job/ home/ someone to love; learn new skills, set new records, create new things; or change their life in any other way.

It's not unfair to use any of these methods to achieve our dreams. It's not unfair to use manifestation work to do this either. It's just another way of getting where you're going – and for folks who worry that energy work is unfair because it's "secret and only a few folk know it", there are plenty of references, including this one, available, and anyone can use these methods to help themselves along their journey.

Anyone can do it- and that makes it fair.

There are some times when manifestation can be unethical if you do it the wrong way. Unethical manifestation can make energy bounce back at you in a negative manner and give you grief, so it's something to avoid. Let's look at how that works, so we can avoid doing it, and causing the problems in our lives.

There are two primary ways that we can unethically do manifestation:

- When we mean to harm someone or unfairly take something of theirs during manifestation; and
- When we use manifestation work to try to control

someone and interfere with their Free Will.

The basic problem in both of these situations is that we are intentionally choosing to manifest something that we want for ourselves ***specifically*** at the expense of someone else. That's where the problem lies. When we choose to have good things for ourselves, it's usually fine. It's when we choose to take them from someone else to have them for ourselves that we have a problem. For example:

- If we choose to manifest a good job for ourselves, we're fine.
- If we're in competition with someone else for a particular job and we say that "If I am the best person for this job, I am attracting the situation where I am given the job." we're also fine (as long as we deal with the idea that, if someone else is a better fit, the job goes to them.)
- If, on the other hand, we use manifestation work to ensure that we get that job, even though we're not qualified and someone else would be better for it, that's a big problem.
- And, if we use manifestation work to get someone dumped from their job so that we can have it for ourselves, we can end up with even worse results.

It's also a problem when we interfere with the Free Will of other people. That's another way of taking from others to feed our own desires. We steal their lives and turn them into toys for us to play with. For instance:

- If we send out energy to attract someone who'll be a good romantic life partner for us, that's fine.
- If we try to energetically make a specific person fall deeply in love with us, we're interfering with that person's right to choose who to love, and that's unethical.
- If we attempt to metaphysically break a loving couple up so that we can then make one partner our own, that's even worse and the potential for bad results for everyone concerned, especially ourselves, is absolutely staggering.

See how that works? It's acceptable and ethical to ask and work for good things for yourself, whether you're doing it by physical work, energywork or just changing your approach to things. It's unethical when you use energywork to coerce someone or directly harm them.

It works pretty much like everything else in life does.

In the previous section, I talked about how it's ethical to manifest good things for yourself, but not to limit, coerce or harm others through energywork.

There is one exception to this rule. It is ethical to use energywork to protect yourself or those you care for from the bad acts of others. When you or people you care for are threatened, whether physically, mentally, emotionally or financially, it's acceptable to use manifestation to deflect or fend off such an assault.

As we say at my house "Your right to swing your fist ends at the tip of my nose."

There are parameters for using energy work for defense.

- You should not prevent an attack by a counter attack. (It's not ok to deal with the guy who calls you names every day by manifesting the measles for him.)
- No overkill. (You cannot respond to someone who parks in handicapped parking spaces with a car fire.)
- You need to use the minimum interference with the other person's Free Will possible. (For the terminally nasty boss, it's not acceptable to give her a personality makeover, but its fine to attract a positive, supportive work place for you and let the Universe sort that one out itself.)
- If you can find a positive method to deflect danger, that's the best option. (For the unpleasant gentleman at work, perhaps you could attract a better job for him at another facility…a facility far, far away…)
- Failing a positive method, a neutral one is the preferable choice. (Such as when that depressed cousin who keeps you on the phone for hours and drains your strength suddenly finds a new interest, and has less time for draining phone calls.)
- And, remember, not getting everything you want does not constitute a threat to you. (You're only permitted to deflect direct harm, not use this as a rationale for marching over the top of other people

in metaphysical hob nailed boots.)

These parameters are a bit like the martial arts. You want to avoid controlling other people, using only the minimum interference to prevent them from harming you.

Please also note that, while it's all right to use energywork to protect people you care for from harm, this doesn't include preventing them from doing something to themselves that you see as harmful. Since everyone's different, it's easy for one person to see an act as positive and another to see the same act as "self-destructive" or "dumb". That's a slippery slope, because it can lead you into trying to dictate how someone else should live his life. Interfering with someone else's Free Will is one of the best ways possible to attract negative energy and negative experiences to follow.

You might like to save someone from something you see as pain or problems. To do that, you're entitled to talk to them, educate them, wheedle them, nag them and even give them consequences; but the moment you start to try to control them energetically, you actually lose control over the situation and make things worse. Save the energywork for safety while they learn things, and coming to the best resolution possible.

To keep your energywork ethical, one good thing to incorporate is a qualifier statement for manifesting what you want. For instance:

- If I am the best person for this job, they will hire

me.
- If it would be good for me to travel abroad, I will get an invitation to go.
- If this person would be a good partner for me, when I invite them to go out, they will say yes.

We may think that we know what would make us happy, but sometimes we're wrong, and statements like these shape reality to support us if the long term benefits would be positive, as well as prevent us from entering a situation that would really be better for someone else.

We've looked at some beliefs about ethics in manifestation. We've looked at some limiting beliefs, and why they don't have to limit us. We've looked at how it's fine to ask for good things for ourselves as long as we don't do it with the intent to penalize others.

Let's look at one last way we can keep our manifestation ethical - the use of a statement about the highest good in our manifestation.

In ethical manifestation work, we're working with four principals:

- It's ethical to ask for good things for ourselves.
- It's not ethical to hurt others in the process of getting good things for ourselves.
- We don't always know what will work out to be good for ourselves or others.
- It's possible for everyone to win in the process.

This means that what looks like our dream job now may end up turning into the Job of Doom. If someone else was also in the running for that job and they lost it to us, they not only benefit from not getting the Job of Doom, but may also be therefore in that position to pick up the Really-Good-Job because they didn't get the first one. Finally, it's possible for both us and our rivals to bypass the Job of Doom, and end up in better jobs instead.

Nifty, eh?

Sometimes, it's good to know what you want and ask for it - but it's also usually good to leave wiggle room for the Universe to give you what you're looking for in ways that you haven't even thought of. It's also good to build in a statement that supports the happiest ending possible for everyone in the situation; and that's where a highest good statement comes in. A highest good statement is a safety net for your energy work to prevent unforeseen problems. It opens the door to even better things than you originally requested. It blesses you and your rivals as well.

A highest good statement incorporates several parts:

- A statement that opens the way for even better solutions than you've thought of (your wiggle room);
- A statement that the solution will be for the higher good of all concerned (which prevents your good harming others and channels energy into a positive solution for them as well);
- An acknowledgment that the process is already underway (which builds belief and puts energy in motion),

and
- A statement of gratitude. (This last is optional, but gratitude is positive energy that makes things happen.)

There's quite a lot of ways to put these pieces together. When I'm doing manifestation work, at the end, I always like to add the statement:

"...I ask for this or something better for the highest good of all concerned and I give thanks that this is happening as I speak..."

This covers all of the pertinent points, and automatically keeps my work positive and ethical. You're welcome to use my statement, or develop your own that supports both abundance and the highest good of all.

Once you have created your statement, it may feel awkward at first. I'd urge you to practice it and use it until it becomes second nature to you. It will help keep your energywork on the right track.

In the end, your beliefs often determine what's right to do with manifestation and what isn't, and there's a lot of variability amongst people on the subject. That's something that you'll need to decide for yourself to get started.

I find the basics in manifestation are:

- It's ethical to help others.

- It's good to treat yourself as well as you do other people.
- It's ok to ask for good things for yourself.
- It's not ok to try to hurt or control others.
- We don't always know how the things we ask for will work out long term.

Using qualifier phrases and highest good phrases can help our manifestation result in positive situations for us and all of the other people involved, and leave room for the Universe to surprise us with even more elegant solutions to what we're asking for.

It's important to do the right thing, both because it affects the kind of person we are and also the world around us. When you're doing manifestation, please do that work ethically and don't break someone else's rice bowl when you're filling your own.

Chapter 7
Choosing a Technique

What's the best technique for manifesting what you want in your life? The bad news is there's no set answer to that. The good news is also that there's no set answer to that. Since everyone is unique, different and special, everyone's beliefs and approaches to manifestation work will be unique too. When doing your type of manifestation, you'll have lots of things to consider.

- Is there a deadline or a time factor involved? Can you make this objective happen gradually over time, or will "really bad things" happen if you don't hit your goal by Tuesday next?
- Are you headed for a specific goal, or is your objective more loosely defined and open to a number of different ways of achieving it?
- Do you have a lot of free time to do manifestation work in, or is your working time limited?
- Besides the total amount of time you have to work on this, how is that time broken up? Can you do this in one big chunk or do you have to spread it out in little bits throughout your day? (And which way do you prefer to work, for that matter?)
- Have you done preparation work? Are you willing to do preparation work?
- Do you have a manifestation buddy to work with, or are you flying solo? Is there any way you could find a partner to work with? (Some techniques are more powerful if you work with someone else.)

- And, most of all, which techniques feel awkward to you and which feel as warm and comfy as a favorite sweater? (Yes, even if you've never done them before, some of these methods may feel like coming home...)

Everybody's going to have a favorite. Everybody's going to have one of these that they wouldn't touch with a ten foot pole. Besides that, any of these methods can cause resistance, and there's no clear answer on which one will and which one won't. It's based on what pushes your buttons or smoothes your personal path. On top of all of that, you'll find that a technique may be perfect for one situation, and not so good for another. The bottom line is that there are great techniques here, but there are no perfect ones - just the one that's perfect (or at least good enough) for right now. For that reason, what I'd recommend for the best results is that you try all of them for yourself, so you have a working knowledge of them.

Yep, that's right. Try all of them. You can skip any ones you really don't want to do, but I'd still say that it's best to try each and every one of them at least once.

Play with them. Try starting out using them for things that would be nice but that you aren't heavily invested in, like nicer weather, less traffic on your trip or getting that phone call back today. Don't wait to play with manifestation until your need is great and your situation dire. Do it now when things are (hopefully) more positive and at peace. Take time to play with each technique in a spirit of gentle experimentation. As you play with them, watch for things like this:

- Which techniques come more easily to you? Which ones don't? You may still find yourself using the more challenging ones at times, but the ones that feel natural will demand less of you, and that's important in times of stress or crisis.
- Which techniques work better with your personal schedule and lifestyle? Is it easier for you to be saying affirmations during your drive to work or making a big block of time on the weekend to clean house and Feng Shui your world?
- Which ones seem to trigger your resistance? Sometimes that's just a question of getting used to the technique, but it's worth noting.
- Pay attention to what your body is telling you– what your neck, your back, your shoulders, the pit of your stomach and any other pertinent parts of your body have to say. Like stress, resistance is often felt first by what our bodies tell us, and the methods that activate resistance may not be your first go-to techniques.
- Listen to your thoughts and emotions, too. Watch for the signs of resistance you identified earlier.
- Which ones do you see a more immediate result with? Which ones seem to take more time before things start happening for you?
- Which ones just work better for you? Which ones don't?

Some of these methods may feel more natural or useful or workable for you than others. It's certainly ok to have your favorites - a string of preferred techniques you habitually use when you need to make things happen; but don't count the others out because they're not currently speaking to you.

As I said above, I'd recommend that you try them all at least once, even the ones that seem less likely to work for you. Make yourself familiar with them all, and then, when you want to do manifestation work, you'll have a better feel for what may work best for you. The one thing that's guaranteed is that your situation will eventually change and the method that seems clunky and awkward today may be just what you need a week from Tuesday. You owe it to yourself to be familiar with your options, even if you only choose to use some of them.

If you get to the point where that least likely exercise is the one that's the proper combination of power and discretion you need to shift the world around you, you'll be glad you took the time to get to know it.

Once you're familiar with the different techniques, you'll know which ones you prefer and be ready to work. Remember though, as noted above, your favorites may not be the best choice on every occasion. When you start doing manifestation work, pay attention. If you start feeling signs of resistance, that's a message that this particular method may be great, but still not the right one for this time. At that point, consider either dropping back and going slower (ask for less, repeat technique less frequently, etc.) or possibly even stop and try a different method.

Sometime there's resistance no matter what method

you use. Look at what you're asking for, and if there's a good reason not to have it. If your goal is ethical and appropriate, then you may just be working through your own negative programming, and may have to face some resistance before you come out the other side.

In Appendix I at the back of the book, I've got a chart that may help you figure out which techniques might better meet your needs, but remember that it's still important to try them all. When choosing the right method of manifestation work, the bottom line is that there is no one "right" method. What's right is what works best for you, for your beliefs, for your schedule, and for your lifestyle. When you listen to what your inner wisdom tells you, you'll find the right technique every time.

Chapter 8
Making Manifestation a Part of Your Life

You've set an intention and chosen a technique to achieve it. Now it's time to figure out how that technique fits into your life.

In metaphysics, there's no "one size fits all". Some techniques are quick, and some take more time. Some you do once, and some require repetition. Different people need different methods, and the technique that works best for your friend is not always the one that's best for you. Indeed, the method that worked great for you last week may be "just wrong" today.

You've chosen a technique and that's good. This chapter is about how to make it work – about the basics of working a manifestation practice, and fitting it into your life, so you can get the best possible use out of different techniques.

While manifestation may create things that save you time and effort in the long run, it's important to remember that in the short run you'll have to invest some time and effort to get that work to do something. At this point, one thing you may want to think about is how much time and effort different techniques need.

Some manifestation processes are one shot affairs. You clear a space in your schedule, you do them once and then you're done. On the other hand, many of them involve multiple sessions, or making a change of an ongoing or permanent nature. Some of them are lengthy, and are better when broken into smaller parts that can be done one at a time as your schedule permits.

Because of this, it's worth looking at your personal habits and schedule, and figuring out where manifestation fits into everything else you're trying to do in your life.

- Are you a night owl? You might want to do your manifestation when everyone else is asleep.
- More of a morning lark? The early hours are for you.
- Busy after work? Could you clear a day on a weekend to do a bigger technique, like Feng Shui?
- Busy all of the time? Chose a method that can be broken into little bits and pieces, and done on breaks or in little bits of time throughout the day.

It's not only important to choose the process that appeals to you, but also one that suits your life style; and then build it into your schedule.

If you have a process with multiple steps or that must be done on a regular basis, you'll need to build a manifestation routine, and follow it regularly. Create situational cues that remind you to do the work. Put notes in places where you'll see them to remind yourself to do your manifestation.

If your environment and routine support incorporating manifestation throughout your life, it'll be easier and more natural to do.

When thinking about how often to do manifestation work, people take a couple of different approaches.

For some methods, the more attention you put on your goal or intention, the more energy you're channeling into your manifestation. With these particular techniques, it's important to do them multiple times, and a regular schedule may help.

In other practices, you're expected to do them once, and then let them go, confident that they're coming together. To do those practices multiple times implies a lack of confidence that the process will work. Through the mind-body connection, that belief weakens the process and makes it less likely to succeed.

In the field of manifestation, some folks believe that a "the more/the better" process is the way things always work; while others go with "ask once and detach." I believe that this varies based on the process, and that your situation may also affect things as well.

Whether you believe in one approach or the other or a little bit of both is up to you. As we know, what you believe tends to shape the reality around you, so be sure to choose what works with your life

---

When you're doing manifestation work, it's very likely that you may want to do more than one process at a time.

There are several steps to manifestation, and different processes work on different steps. Some make your energy more positive, making it easier to attract things you want. Some are ways of asking for what you want.

Some bolster belief in the process and help you prepare to receive what you're asking for. Some are good for more than one step.

What technique or techniques you chose depend on what you're trying to accomplish and the situation you're in.

- Are you now facing challenges, stress, or adversity, and doing manifestation work to improve your situation? Check yourself for signs of negativity or negative energy. If you find some (and it isn't surprising if you do), you may want to start with methods for raising the level of your energy and making it more positive. This makes manifestation easier, and reduces your chance of resistance.
- To manifest something you want, you have to ask for it. As they say "If you don't ask, you don't get." A manifestation technique for asking is an essential step.
- The more you believe that manifestation can work, the easier it is to do it. Especially at first, you may want to use a process that supports your belief that manifestation work is real. If that's too much at once, you at least need to support that it *might* work. Techniques for improving your energy can help with this, but sometimes you may want a method that directly supports belief in the process.
- Finally, you need to prepare to receive what you're manifesting. The actions of preparing for a new reality in the expectation that it is on the way speeds that reality into your life.

If you're using multiple practices, you may or may not want to be working on them at the same time. You may want to exclusively work a technique to improve your energy until you feel like your vibes are right, and then move on to a technique for asking. On the other hand, you may want to do your method for asking first thing when you get up in the morning and scatter methods of improving your energy throughout your day.

Trust your instincts. Choose what flows for you, and remember if it becomes challenging, it may be time to revise your practice. Whichever ways feel good to you and work with your lifestyle are the right ones for your unique life.

We've talked about resistance in previous chapters. Indeed, you might want to choose techniques by which triggers resistance and which don't; but resistance pops up in manifestation in another way. In processes that take place over time, you may find that techniques that work well at first may start to trigger resistance as you go along. This can happen when your manifestation's moving fast enough to slide into a zone your unconscious finds uncomfortable or scary. The unconscious may unleash resistance then to alert you that you're going into hazardous territory or to try to get you to back up into a more familiar reality.

If you're not paying attention, this can make you feel uncomfortable without knowing why. It can also partially or totally block your manifestation work. If you're paying attention, though, you have options. You can choose to slow down on the manifestation you're doing, or even switch to another process that doesn't stimulate as much resistance.

When we talked about resistance, we looked at the physical, mental and emotional signals of resistance unique to you. Since you know them, you're now able to watch out for them. When you're doing manifestation work over time, watch for those signals of resistance, and use them as a heads up that you may need to adjust your process.

In the end, people have their own unique lives, and particular needs and limitations to go with that. Because of this, there's no one clear and perfect way for the perfect manifestation practice. That's the bad news - and the good news is that there are as many different ways to manifest things as people having needs.

To build the manifestation practice that's perfect for you, you need to look at your own personal time, needs and tastes, and select methods that fit into your life. You need to be alert and aware, and adjust your methods as needed as your own energy shifts. Finally, you need to stick with your practice, in order to change reality in your little corner of the cosmos. When you've laid the groundwork and done the work, you'll begin to see things happen.

We're finished now with the foundations of manifestation. It's time to move forwards into the practices, and let you choose the ones that suit your tastes. See you in the next section.

THE PROCESSES

Preparing Your Energy

Chapter 9
On Preparing Your Energy Field

I had finally completed the two chapters I'd been struggling with, and was feeling pretty good about that. I decided to celebrate by going to my local coffee shop. I'm a coffee wimp and like drinks with a lot of chocolate and a little coffee, and I just happened to have a coupon for a dollar off my beverage of choice.

At checkout, the nice young kid behind the counter took my coupon and then turned to me with a confused but happy look on his face "I know the coupon says $1 off" he said "but it's taken the whole thing off."

I asked if that was o.k. (I didn't want to get him in trouble.) He said "The register has spoken." and grinned at me.

I walked in with good energy. I walked out with even better energy, a sense of wonder and a free frozen mocha...

As I said in the first part of this book, like calls to like. Because of this, if you want to manifest positive things, it's much easier to do if you start out with a positive energy field. While you can be somewhat down and still manifest positive things, it's much harder work that way.

The processes in this section will help you bring your energy up, and help keep it that way. They're not a guarantee you'll always be happy and your energy positive, but if you practice one or more on a regular basis, you'll find your outlook tends to be more positive and your energy too. Regular practice will also make it easier to notice when events move you in a cranky direction, and to move yourself back to your happy place.

Sometimes keeping your energy field positive is enough to draw positive things into your life. Pay attention as you work with these processes and see if that happens. If your energy is positive enough, that may be all you need to attract prosperity.

Sometimes your energy may be running at a good level without your having to do anything special. Stop a moment and listen to your energy. Do you feel any negativity? Do you feel any resistance?

If you don't, you may want to skip this step, and go straight to asking for what you want; or you may want to do an energy process anyway to keep your energy positive and possibly move it a little higher.

Good enough is good enough.

Positive energy is the first step on the way to manifestation. It supports your health in body, mind and spirit; and it feels good too. If you're not generating it spontaneously, it's worth the time and effort to get yourself to this level and keep yourself there.

Let's look at different ways to make your energy more positive.

Chapter 10
The "My Favorite Things" Toolkit

We want to manifest positive things in our lives, and having a positive energy field makes that much easier. One big question then is how do you develop a positive energy field and keep it that way?

For the most part, the nature of your energy field is set by the things that you focus on. If you spend most of your time concentrating on what you don't have and what's wrong with your life, these negative thoughts tend to drag your energy down to a more negative level. If, on the other hand, you spend more time focusing on more positive things, your energy likewise becomes more positive, and more magnetic to bring what you want into your life.

If your outlook tends to be positive, keeping your energy field positive is less of a problem. You focus on positive things, and the energy from that tends to attract more positive things, which means that, (short of any unexpected catastrophes), your energy field and your life mutually support each other.

What happens, though, if a crisis happens and pulls you into negative thinking patterns; or if you've developed a more negative, cynical focus on the world around you?

It's understandable if having negative experiences leads you to having a more negative view of the world. Unfortunately, the more your emotions, thoughts and beliefs go there, the more negative your energy field can become and the more negative things you can attract.

What's the answer to that? How do you keep from getting stuck in a negative cycle?

One way to break a negative cycle is something I call the "My Favorite Things" toolkit. This kit is simple to put together, but useful for heading off negative energy and maintaining a more positive energetic level.

All you need for the tool kit are three simple items:

- A list of things you're grateful for, or that make you feel happy thinking about them,
- A list of things to do that make you feel happy, and
- The actual things that make you feel happy

That's all you need, so let's get started on this.

It's better to put this kit together when you're feeling positive. (It's easier to come up with things that help you to feel good or happy when you don't have the blues.) In a pinch, you can pull this together at any time, even if you're going through challenges in your life.

Start by making a list of things you're grateful for or that you feel happy thinking about.

- Sunny weather.
- Skiing
- A silly hat.

These can be deep and symbolic things like "having my health" or "a good relationship", or things that seem trivial but still lift your spirits, such as a certain pop song or hot fudge sundaes. You'll know that something belongs on this list if you get a smile on your face or a warm feeling in your heart when it first occurs to you. Don't worry if some of the things on your list seem silly or childish – this list is just for you, and you won't be graded or judged on it, so enjoy yourself.

Make as long of a list as you can, and include a variety of things on it, because different types of things lift your spirits at different times.

The next step is to make a second list of things that you can do that make you feel happy.

- Singing
- Shopping
- The scent and feel of a particular hand lotion as you apply it.

This should also involve a variety of choices, as something may work at one point, where a different time may need a totally different practice. Be sure to include options that take a short amount of time, a small amount of effort or little to no money, as there will always be times in life when you need a pickup but money, time or energy are in short supply.

Don't just *think* about these things now while you're in a good space. Make sure to write them down, and keep copies of both of these lists in places where you have easy access to them and will see them often. The point of doing this now is that, when you're feeling more positive, it's easier to come up with lists of this kind of things, but when you're down, it's harder to remember that there are any good things in life at all.

Be prepared to add to both of these lists as you go through life and find more things that uplift you. (Keeping a master copy on your computer is not a bad thing.)

Finally, to complete your kit, have supplies for activities that lift your mood in stock and ready to use so they're easily available to you.

- A funny or inspiring book.
- Soap in a scent that makes you feel good.
- A recording of music that energizes you.

Don't put yourself in a position where it's one in the morning, you can feel your energy slipping downwards, and you can't put your hands on the inspirational recording or slice of cheesecake that would turn everything around until the stores open the following day. Always try to have the supplies you need for several types of positive energy building available to you and ready to go when you need them.

If you're having problems figuring out what things you should put on your lists or in your kit, having one or more people help you plan this energetic tool can be helpful. If we're out of the habit of doing nice things for ourselves, we can actually lose track of what we like and what makes us happy, and get stuck when the question comes up.

Be sure to choose people who know you well, who you know care about you and who have your best interests at heart. Two heads can be better than one, and a trusted friend or loved one may have good insight into the things that make you happy but that you're currently overlooking.

Now you've got your favorite things toolkit. What do you do with it?

There are two primary ways that you can use your toolkit.

- You can use it like a first aid kit when you're feeling negative and low, to help you to re-focus on more positive things, to return your energy to a more positive state,
and
- You can use it like vitamins to help maintain and improve your positive energy.

Pretty versatile, eh? Let's look at to how do this.

Let's look at emergency intervention first. Anyone can have a bad hair day, or challenging times, or get smacked in the face by an unexpected crisis, or have a day that's like being nibbled to death by baby ducks. It happens to us all, and it's not wrong to feel blue, overwhelmed or ticked off when it does happen.

What do we do to move our energy back up into the more positive range? How can we use our favorite things toolkit to help us do this?

- We can start by looking at the list of things that make us feel happy or grateful. We already have positive feelings connected with these things and shifting our attention from things that stress us to things that make us happy is often enough to send our energy spiraling upwards again.
- We can look at the second list and pick something to do that will help move us back to the positive side of the scale. It's important to pick something we can do now or soon, as activities set in the future have less power to help us change.
- We can pick one of the items that make us feel happy and use it now. Set the table with the pretty china, rather than waiting for the holidays. Go to the movies tonight. Don't save that expensive hand crème for a special occasion - use it now. Making an effort to nurture yourself promptly and regularly makes you feel special and valued and tends to shift your energy to a positive state.

Using your toolkit when you first notice you're feeling down can help you start feeling better at once and keep you from sliding further downwards energetically

---

.

We've talked about the toolkit as a remedy for the blues. Now, let's look at it as a preventative. How can you use this tool to prevent negative energy?

- You can review the list of things that make you feel happy or grateful on a regular basis. Take a moment

during the day to just read down the list and think about one or two of the list items, noticing how you feel when you do this. As we know, what we give our attention to set the vibration for our energy, so choosing to focus on positive things helps our energy stay positive.
- Schedule time to do things on the second list of things that make you feel happy when you do them. If a regular trip to the movies, massage, or smoothie will help keep your energy positive, don't just wait and see if you happen to have time to do them. Book specific times to do them and treat those commitments to yourself as being as important as your commitments to other people are.
- Be sure that some of your toolkit supplies are things you can use throughout your busy schedule, then build your schedule so it includes positive moments throughout your routine. Don't just go for special occasions, like dinner out or a trip to the movies. Fill your day with little dots of happy, like pretty stamps, extra comfortable slippers or personal theme music cued up on your music system. When happy pervades your day, your energy is more likely to stay positive, even when bumps in the road come along.

Your toolkit serves as a cue and a reminder that there are positive things in the world to focus on, as well as basic equipment to help us head in that direction.

You'll find your toolkit is both flexible and helpful to you, empowering you to keep your energy positive and to get it back there when things knock you out of kilter. Use your toolkit not only as emergency treatment for a bad hair day, but also as a system to keep your focus primarily positive ranges, and you'll find it much easier to manifest the kind of things that you want.

Chapter 11
The "What If Things Got Better" Technique?

Start with the idea that positive energy attracts positive things into our lives and makes it easier for us to manifest them as we choose. Go on by understanding that our emotions are a strong part of determining our energy levels, and that positive feelings and a positive attitude have a major effect on our energy. Going further, let's acknowledge that positive energy and positive emotions just feel good.

Given all of that, why would anyone voluntarily head off into negativity?

The number one reason that people make negative energy for themselves is worry and anxiety; and one of the biggest reasons that people experience these emotions is a little game I call "what if things got worse?" People play this game by telling themselves stories about terrible things that might possibly happen in the future, and then worrying like mad about these things, dragging their energetic levels downwards.

- What if I never find anyone to love me?
- What if the economy crashes and my savings are completely wiped out?
- What if I come down with some kind of terminal illness?

This game is seductive to people because it's made up of both truth and of lies. The truth is the fact that the things people worry about are vaguely possible - but the lies are that most of these things rarely happen, if ever. These are the kind of things that are only worthy of worry if you have concrete evidence that they're actually happening. By worrying about them when there's no sign that they're actually happening, you make yourself suffer and trash your energy for things that aren't currently real in your life, and may never be.

Try this "what if things got worse?" game for yourself right now. Take a moment, and pay attention to what your energy feels like when you're not worrying.

Once you're aware of how your energy feels, tell yourself a "what if things got worse?" story about something that concerns or worries you. Check in with your energy again.

Note the difference? Most people find themselves feeling tired, drained, exhausted or down after playing "what if things got worse?", and it can do even more damage if you have a bunch of friends or co-workers that like to play it with you.

This way of thinking exhausts us physically, leaving us without the resources to actually do anything to avoid negative experiences or create good ones. On top of that, it spirals our energy downwards into the negative levels; and we all know that negative energy makes us more likely to attract negative things into our lives.

Not a very useful game, "What if things got worse?"…

....but fortunately, we have other options.

We can play "what if things get better?"

Instead of dreading a future where things go badly, we can instead lay the groundwork for a time to come when things improve in our lives.

- What if love is waiting just around the corner?
- What if the economy continues to improve and my personal finances get better and better?
- What if my body is strong and healthy and stays that way?

When we tell ourselves positive things, we improve our energy, which makes it easier to manifest a better reality and we also energize ourselves physically as well, which puts us in a better position to accomplish things on the physical plane.

It's time to try this version. Just as you did in the previous section, notice how your energy feels at a neutral level, and then make a "What if things got better?" statement.

Notice how your energy feels when you make that statement? Mine tends to feel positive and expansive when I'm asking "What if things got better?" and each question that I ask gives me more strength and positive energy, that I can use to help things happen. Indeed, a good session of "What if things got better?" can leave me feeling giggly and energized and ready to go out and Do Great Things.

When you first start playing with this, you may want to start small.

- What if I did very well in the talent contest tomorrow?
  As opposed to
- What if I won the talent contest, was spotted by a talent scout from Hollywood and was whisked away to sign a contract to star in a minimum of three movies?

Too big a "What if things got better?", especially when you're just starting out, can trigger resistance, which cuts the effectiveness of the technique.

On the other hand, it's very effective to start small and work rapidly upwards in steps.

- What if I did very well in the talent contest tomorrow?
- What if I won that contest?
- What if winning meant I appeared in the paper?
- What if a Hollywood talent scout saw that article, and dropped by to audition my act?
- What if he were impressed by my talent, and got me an interview at the studios?
- What if I aced that interview and got hired to act in films?
- What if my acting career took off, and I ended up as a film star?

Taking that sequence step by step increases your energy a little bit with each level but tends not to trigger resistance, and you can do a string of these back to back while dancing around the mental blocks your subconscious may have built.

As you become more experienced with this technique, you'll find that you can handle bigger and bigger jumps without blinking an eye.

Once you get the hang of the basic process, start listening to yourself and the stories you tell yourself. Catch yourself when you start to warn yourself of catastrophes that may or may not arrive.

- What if I'm late for my appointment?
- What if I verbally stumble during my interview and look like a fool?
- What if they don't like me?

Instead of catastrophizing, try asking yourself "What if it got better?"

- What if I arrive right on time?
- What if I do perfectly during my interview?
- What if I am just who they want for the job?

Stop shooting yourself in the foot. Instead, start re-training yourself to tell yourself stories that empower you, improve your energy and manifest a better world for yourself.

Make a habit of "What if things got better?"

"What if things got better?" is a great game to play on your own, but it's even better fun to play with someone else.

- What if my article was accepted for publication?
- *What if your article was accepted for publication in a national magazine?*
- What if it was published in a national magazine and I got paid for it?
- *What if you got paid a lot of money for it?*
- What if that publication led to other writing jobs for me?
- *What if you became the national "go-to" author on your subject and you had magazines fighting over your work?*

When you use this process with a partner, you tend to play off of each other and raise that "what ifs?" to bigger and bigger levels. A "What if?" buddy will also think of things that you might not think of yourself, and say things that you're too shy or embarrassed to say out loud because they seem too outrageous.

See if you can find someone who'd be willing to play "What if things got better?" with you.

It's useful to have a buddy to play "What if things got better?" with. It's even better if you can get a group to do it.

Build yourself a group of caring people, who can be trusted to be supportive of each other. Teach them the basic "What if things got better?" process; then set them up in a circle, with each member taking a turn in the center. Set a time limit, so everybody gets a chance to be in the center.

The center person gives a topic or concern that could use the application of positive energy; and then the other members take turns applying "What if things got better?" statements to it. Dependant on what works best for your group, you can either go around and let each person take a turn or do it free style as people are moved to do so.

Either way, this can generate an amazing amount of positive energy in a relatively short amount of time.

"What if things got better?"

What a deceptively simple concept, but making this your focus can bring your energy levels to the point where they attract good things and things indeed get better.

That's worth thinking about the next time that you tell yourself a story.

Chapter 12
Manifestation at Home

You'd like to manifest better things in your life. Unfortunately, there seem to be an awful lot of other things piling up on your "To Do" list as well. It's sometimes hard to find time to do a complex manifestation practice on top of everything else you've got going on. That's one of the reasons this book is about simpler manifestation techniques. They usually don't take as much time and effort, or they take small amounts of it throughout the day, so they're a lot easier to work into your schedule. Wouldn't it be great though if you could combine manifestation work with something else you need to do?

Well, this is the chapter where you can do just that.

In metaphysics, there's a law sometimes known as the Law of Association. It basically says that when you have two things with elements in common, what you do to one can affect the other. This means that, when you have a thing that symbolizes another, working energetically on the first one can affect the second. When working with energy, you can get a lot of mileage out of symbolic work, and many people have done so throughout history.

If you're going to use the Law of Association as part of your manifestation practice, you'll need something that stands for or symbolizes you and your life. There are lots of different things used for this at different times in history (pictures, dolls, your signature, etc.) so you have plenty of options to choose from. What's one of the better things you can use to symbolize yourself and your life when trying to manifest things you want?

Your home....

When you live in a place long enough that it's your home, you develop an energetic connection with your space that has metaphysical potential. One illustration of this is the story of the vampire who cannot come in a home unless the people who live there invite him in. The house, once it becomes a home, also becomes an extension of the people who live there, and its threshold has protection against intrusions from those not invited in by the residents.

The connection applies when the place you live is your home, whether you own that place or rent it. These connections don't usually work as well for hotel rooms or any other type of temporary lodging (although there are ways around this), but the connection between a true home and its inhabitants is real and can be useful in energy work.

When you're working with the energy of the connection between you and your home, there are some basic things you need to know at the start.

1) Clutter can block the energy of a space and how it flows. Ever notice how when things "pile up", the air and the energy of that space starts to feels stale and stagnant and dead? Have you noticed how, when you clear things out and put things away, you begin to feel energized again?

Part of that's the psychological effects of clutter and how that effects the mind - body connection, but part of that's how actual physical clutter interacts with the energy of a space. While a limited amount of disorder can be workable, too much clutter, especially long-term clutter, can begin to have an effect on that energy.

In addition, many times a buildup of clutter can also be symbolic (there's those symbols again!) of areas needing attention in our own lives.

2) Blocked energy tends to be stagnant, draining or negative. When the energy of a space is blocked and no longer moving freely, it tends to become stale and stagnant. People in that space can feel tired, uninspired or depressed. In the long term, it can even affect your personal energy and health.

3) At any point in time, clearing the clutter can improve the energy of the space, and therefore the things that you attract into your life.

There's good news about this though, and it comes in three parts.

1) You don't have to be perfect (which is a relief for me and probably for most of us.)

2) It's never too late to use cleaning and de-cluttering to have a positive effect on the energy of your space. Even if that closet has been full of old mementos of your high school days for 20 years, sitting down now and weeding out things you don't really want anymore can have a positive effect on your space's energy.

3) You don't have to do everything. Even starting with a drawer, a bookshelf or a corner of the room can make a difference.

There's a number of ways to work with your home

to improve your energy, but in this chapter, we're going to be looking at two – setting an intention, and Feng Shui. Let's get started…

The simplest way to do manifestation work while you clean your house is to set an intention As you may recall from Chapter three, that's just a fancy term for setting a goal so that the energy of house cleaning powers your manifestation.

How do you set an intention while you clean?

You start just before you start your housecleaning task, whether it's doing dishes, de-cluttering, or cleaning the bathroom sink. You make a statement that boils down to "Out with the old and in with the new." in its simplest form. Where it's possible, it's good to match the task with what you're trying to achieve. For instance:

- "As I clear out this closet, I also clear out old patterns of behavior that kept me stuck in meaningless employment and I open my life to better jobs that fulfill me."
- "As I wash gunk off of these dishes, I also wash the gunk out of my beliefs, clearing the way for more positive beliefs and a more positive reality."
- "As I clear my closet of old clothes that no longer fit, I also clear old relationships that also don't fit and open my life to a loving and caring partner."

It's good to include words indicating that you're letting go of negative things or things that no longer serve you, and bringing in things that you'll be happier with to point towards the results you want.

You can set an intention silently or out loud, based on what works best for you and who else is around who might be disconcerted by the process. For some people, saying it out loud gives it more power, but I find that it works well either way.

As you wash those dishes, or clean that closet, or mop that floor, you focus of course on the process of cleaning, but you also want to keep your mind on your energetic intention, to send the energy generated by cleaning to that goal. As the act of cleaning changes what is being cleaned, you make a mental and energetic link between that change and the change you want in your world, and the focus helps to slant reality towards that change coming into reality.

When you finish your cleaning project, sit back for a moment and take a good look at what you've physically accomplished. At that point, feel gratitude for the other good things that will soon also be present in your life.

That's it. That's really all you need to do. And you even got the dishes clean in the process…

We'll be going further into setting an intention and different ways you can use that in manifestation in another chapter coming up, but this section gives you enough of the basics to use with housecleaning to make the energy around you more positive so that manifesting positive things is easier and quicker.

Combining setting an intention with household

chores is a simple, time efficient way to do manifestation, but there's another way you can work with your home to make your energy better for manifestation.

Feng Shui is the Chinese practice also known as "the way of wind and water". It goes back in history to at least 6000 B.C. Feng Shui is a very complex practice, but the basic definition of it is the art of arranging objects, buildings and space to achieve energy, harmony and balance. Chinese philosophy says everything is made up of energy or "chi". When the flow of energy is free and unfettered, everything goes well and we have prosperity, health and happiness in our lives. When the flow is somehow blocked, this leads to undesirable experiences such as illness, poverty and loss.

To restore a good life, we need to do things that unblock blocked chi and let it flow freely once again. In a person's body, we use accupressure or acupuncture to clear the blocked points on the energy meridians and let the chi flow freely. In the environment, we can adjust the placement of furniture and other items, or apply things called Feng Shui "cures" to compensate for items that cause blockages that cannot be moved or otherwise realigned.

There is far more to the art of Feng Shui than we can cover in the rest of this chapter or even an entire book. What we'll be looking at in this chapter is the Feng Shui of de-cluttering.

In its simplest form, Feng Shui holds that different areas of your rooms and your house overall stand for different parts of your life. Therefore:

- When dust or clutter or broken items pile up in these areas, they negatively affect the chi of what that area stands for.
- If certain areas tend to accumulate clutter, even when you're trying to correct this, there are ongoing problems in what area symbolizes.
- And when you clean and de-clutter those areas, the thing that area stands for tends to improve as well.

Given what we know about energy and manifestation, this makes sense, right? At that point, if we want to see an improvement in a particular area of our lives, we need to:

- Identify the area of our homes that stands for that thing we wish to improve,
- Look at that area in each room (particularly the bedroom and the office) for things that aren't working, or signs of clutter or dust,
- De-clutter, clean, fix or replace these things(to improve the energy),
and
- Watch things get better in our live as the energy flows freely once more.

That's straight forward enough; but what does each part of the room symbolizes?

Picture each room as being divided into nine segments, like a giant tic-tac-toe board is laid over the top of it. The main entry to the room, whether door or arch, is always in one of the bottom three squares.

Got it? Good. Now, here's what the nine squares stand for.

- The top left square stands for abundance, wealth and prosperity.
- The top square in the middle stands for status, reputation and social standing.
- The top right square stands for loving relationships.
- The middle square on the left stands for roots and ancestors and family.
- The square that's in the middle both vertically and horizontally stands for health and well-being.
- The middle right square stands for creativity and offspring.
- The bottom left square stands for deep wisdom, contemplation, and education.
- The bottom square in the middle stands for your life path and career.
- The bottom square on the right stands for mentors, guardian angels and spirits, and helpful people.

This grid applies both to each individual room, and to the house overall, so look at both spaces. Remember, you enter the room through one of the three bottom squares (Wisdom, Career or Helpful People) so stand in your door way and line the grid up from there. When you're looking at individual rooms, the places that have the most impact are the bedroom and the place in your home where you work (home office? Where you sit down to pay the bills?

The desk I'm currently writing at?) Look at those places first.

Now that you know which space means what, how do you apply this?

First, you chose a part of your life that you'd like to see improvement in, and then figure out what areas in that Feng Shui grid might affect this. For instance, if you want to make some progress at your job, you'll want the bottom center square (Career) and, given your circumstances, you might also want to look at top center (Reputation), middle right (Creativity), lower right (Helpful People), or top left (Wealth and Abundance).

Looking at these areas, where do you see clutter? Dust? Broken things? Dead plants?

Once you've spotted your targets, it's time to get to work. Clean, de-clutter, fix or replace things as needed, until the areas are in good, or at least better shape. As you're putting things to rights, keep the intention in your mind that as you straighten things up, you're improving the energy in the space and in the areas of your life that the spaces stand for, and that the better energy will attract better things into that area of your life.

When you're done, sit back and enjoy the results, both in a cleaner house and in better energy that brings better things into your life.

Remember to keep an eye out for spaces that tend to "draw" clutter. This may just be the convenience of dropping things there, but it can also be a symptom of a bigger trouble spot in your life that you may need to address.

If you find you like Feng Shui, there's a lot more

that you can learn about this art, but we're going to content ourselves with Feng Shui de-cluttering and go onto to other methods of improving your energy to make manifestation easier.

Remember, when you're preparing to do manifestation work, it's good to start by getting your own energy as positive as possible to make yourself more magnetic to the things you want. One good way to do this is to work with the energy of your space, because your home is a symbolic extension of you and your life. Whether you use setting an intention, Feng Shui, or some other way of raising the level of the energy in your home, your space's energy affects your energy; so it's good to look at your home and see what you've given yourself to work with energetically.

Chapter 13
Share the Wealth

We've already looked at several ways to move your energy to the positive vibration that makes it easier to manifest the life you want. Let's look at one more idea that can help improve your energy in order to attract more good things. Let's look at abundance and scarcity beliefs, and at sharing the wealth.

As we know, your beliefs are one thing that determines what kind of energy you're sending out into the universe and therefore what you're attracting back. They create positive or negative energy which draws positive or negative things into your life. They also manifest people, things and experiences in your life in harmony with your beliefs.

In other words, if you're putting out the energy of scarcity, fear and lack, you tend to draw more of that to you. If your energy is more about abundance and gratitude for what you have, you tend to attract more abundance.

To understand this better, let's take a closer look at both scarcity and abundance beliefs.

Earlier in this book, we briefly looked at scarcity beliefs. Scarcity beliefs are one type of programming that makes manifestation more difficult. Some examples of scarcity beliefs are:

- There is never enough money.
- For someone to win, someone else has to lose.

- We are running out of resources.
- I can only succeed at someone else's expense.
- Good things happen to other people, but they never happen to me.

Scarcity beliefs say all resources are limited, and therefore it's hard to get the things you want. There's some truth in that (which can make these beliefs compelling) but the bottom line is that it's only one way of looking at life.

Abundance beliefs, on the other hand, work from the standpoint that the Universe is full of good things and that there's always a way to find the abundance you need or to draw it into your life.

Let's look closer at the idea that there are only finite resources in this world, that they're running out and that we're all in competition for these resources. In its simplest form, think of scarcity in terms of having a communal bag of cookies in the house. With that bag of cookies, we can be afraid that, if our roommate takes two, there won't be enough left for us; or we can work from the standpoint that there are always enough cookies and if we finish this bag, we can just bake some more or go to the grocery and get another bag.

It's true that, at this moment in time, there are only so many cookies/trees/dollars/members of the opposite sex/fill in your choice of favorite things here. It's also true that the Universe is creative, unlimited and generous, and that, as we come to what seems the end of a resource, over and over we find new resources to meet our needs and new ways to find abundance. This happens when we focus more on solutions and being willing to look for them, as opposed to focusing on a situation that seems hopeless. From a psychological standpoint, scarcity beliefs create the expectation that you're going to suffer and fail, where abundance beliefs make you more likely to look for solutions as opposed to just see problems. From a metaphysical standpoint, scarcity beliefs attract scarcity, while abundance beliefs attract abundance.

It's worth noting that there are some concepts that aren't part of abundance beliefs. Abundance beliefs don't mean we should be wasteful of our resources. (That's a kind of arrogance that can lead to more negative things). They don't mean that we should spend money that we don't already have. And they don't mean that someone who is currently financially challenged is automatically to blame in some way for their situation. (This is not a "rich people are good/poor people are bad" philosophy.)

It does mean, however, that, both psychologically and energetically, we consistently do better when we focus on the belief that there are more than enough resources to go around and that the question is how to find and tap into those resources. Abundance beliefs like this keep us focusing on solutions to our challenges. They keep our energy more positive so that it attracts more positive things, opportunities and solutions.

As long as we focus on lack, we draw lack. The situation can turn around once we shift our beliefs and our focus. In the end, it's just more helpful and effective to believe that the Universe is surprisingly unlimited, that there are plenty of good things to go around for everybody, and that believing this helps us to find or manifest them for everyone.

How do you change your beliefs to ones of abundance if you're previously acting from a scarcity mindset? One way is a little process called "Act as if."

To do this, you stop and think. You ask yourself "If my new reality came to pass, how would I act? How would I think? What would I do?"

And then you start to do those things as best you can with the resources that you already have.

Your unconscious mind feels you acting in a new way, and gets the message that this is how things already are. Because the unconscious is very powerful but believes everything you tell it, it immediately sets out to use its power to shape reality to match how you're acting.

Interesting….

There are a number of useful ways to use the "Act as if" process. We'll be talking about more of them later on, but in this chapter, we'll be talking about manifesting money as an example.

How would you act if you had all of the money you needed and then some?

There are a lot of good answers but one of the ones I like best is that you'd have enough money to meet your needs and desires, and still help other people with as well.

Sharing the wealth, whether by tithing, giving to charity or any other ways of sharing your blessings, is a great way to make your world a better place. Interestingly enough, it's also a great way to "Act as if" you're prosperous, change your unconscious beliefs to abundance and attract more good things into your life. When you give, you send the message to the Universe that you have enough to share with others. This is a major "Act as if" and your unconscious tends to work to bring your personal prosperity up to the levels to meet this behavior.

Or, to say this in another way, when you give more, you tend to get more.

This works towards prosperity from several angles.

- When you "act as if" you have enough money to share with other people, your unconscious mind does its best to make that a reality;
- When you focus on the blessings and prosperity you already have, you attract more blessings and prosperity; and
- The act of helping others feels good, which increases the positive vibrations in your energy field, attracting even more good things.

Donating money to someone in need or the cause or charity of your choice is a good thing to do. It also works to improve your energy and helping you manifest positive things from three different angles.

It's worth noting that, when you're sharing the wealth, it doesn't have to be money for this process to work. You can also donate:

- Items (clean out your closet and give someone else

those nice sweaters you're not wearing.)
- Service (offer to stuff envelopes or man a phone.)
- Time (volunteer at a shelter or soup kitchen.)

The Universe is kind of like the I.R.S in this. It gives you credit for all good things you share with those less fortunate than you, and pays your refund in positive energy.

When we share our blessings with those who are less fortunate than ourselves, we set up a chain of energy that blesses ourselves too. We improve our own energy, count our own blessings and invite our unconscious self to see us as prosperous and blessed, and to make that a reality.

It's good to help others for the sake of helping others. It's good to do that with no strings attached, without expecting things in return.

It's also good to know that helping others can improve our own energy and make our own lives better.

Ask

Chapter 14
On Asking

"Ask, and it will be given you…" When it comes to manifestation, we could do much worse than remember this quote from Matthew chapter 7 in the Bible.

While a positive energy field is sometimes enough by itself to attract good things into your life, that's not always the case. To manifest something specific, you'll need to ask for it.

They say you don't get if you don't ask, so what do we need to know about asking?

Asking is the step most likely to trigger resistance in people. It can bring up feelings of unworthiness, fears of being greedy and latent beliefs about good things leading to bad, to mention only three of many blocks out there.

Because of this, it's especially important to monitor yourself for resistance during the "asking" phase. If you use one procedure and start to feel resistance, you have options:

- You can back off and ask for something smaller (reach your goal by steps.) or
- You can try a different procedure.

Fortunately, we've got a number of ways of asking to choose from.

When you're asking to manifest something, you

want to be ethical and not harm someone else in the process. You also want to leave wiggle room for the Universe to give you something even better than you had thought of. For that reason, as discussed in the chapter on ethics, I recommend using a highest good statement, such as:

"...this or something better for the highest good of all concerned"

as part of each request. This keeps your request respectful of others and leaves room for the Universe to surprise and delight you.

Know what you want. Ask for it without triggering resistance. Respect the people and the world around you when you ask. These are the core principles of ethical asking in manifestation work.

This section is about different methods to ask for what you want- to put your request out there to the Universe and let it give you that or something better. Let's look at different ways to do that, and see what suits you.

Chapter 15
The "Wouldn't It Be Nice?" Technique

We're on to asking for what we want now, and the "wouldn't it be nice…" technique is a nice, low energy method for doing this. It's pleasant and even fun to do, it takes little time and can be done in almost any situation, and it's less likely to trigger resistance than almost any other method that I know. If you're trying to manifest change in an area you know you have lots of blocks or resistance in, this is a great technique for that.

The "wouldn't it be nice" technique can be done on your own, but it's also good to do with a partner, as you tend to spur yourself up to greater levels of energy when you're working together as a team. (It's also more fun that way.) Feel free to do it solo, but if you can ring in a manifestation buddy to play this with you, by all means please do so (and more than one buddy makes this even more fun!)

The "wouldn't it be nice…" technique works by asking for something and avoiding triggering resistance in the process by avoiding the direct approach.

As previously said, if your current beliefs and the reality they create are too far removed from what you're trying to manifest, your unconscious mind tends to create resistance as a way of "keeping you safe." Resistance makes it harder to manifest what you want.

A direct statement or command (for instance "Every day in every way, I am getting better and better.") has more power but can often create that resistance. On the other hand, phrasing your request as a "possibility" as opposed to a demand can often bypass resistance, making the entire process work more easily. As one example:

- "My business doubles its income every month" is a very powerful statement, but can trigger resistance in your unconscious. Thoughts like "That's impossible!" start to spring up almost immediately.
- "Wouldn't it be nice if my business doubled its income every month…?" has less direct power, but also mean that you're far less likely to end up fighting against your own unconscious beliefs.

Stop for a moment and try this for yourself. Say or think the first statement (or a similar one on a topic of your choice) and then stop and pay attention to how you feel. Do you feel tension, hesitation, nervousness or resistance? Watch for your signs of resistance that you identified earlier in this book.

Next, try a "wouldn't it be nice….?" statement. Stop again and notice how you're feeling now. You'll probably find that you're more relaxed, and that the feeling of resistance is gone. I find that it feels effortless to me, and it also feels like making that statement opens a door to lots of new possibilities

See how that works? The act of expressing what you're asking for as a pleasant possibility, as opposed to an outright demand, decreases the energy you're putting out to the universe but also decreases the odds of triggering the resistance. Because the less powerful statement doesn't generate resistance to overcome, you may actually achieve your objective more quickly.

How do we create a "wouldn't it be nice statement"?

Start with a statement of what you're trying to achieve. For instance, we could use "My body is always strong and healthy." (Since this is practice, feel free to substitute the statement of your choice, and get a head start on your dreams while learning this process.)

Say your statement out loud, paying attention to how it makes you feel. Do you feel any signs of resistance in your body, energy or emotions? That's a sign that we need to soften this statement to avoid resistance.

Add "wouldn't it be nice" or a similar phrase to your basic statement. Please note that, while I call it the "wouldn't it be nice..." process and usually use the phrase "wouldn't it be nice?" myself, you're not actually tied to use those exact words. Phrases like:

- "What if..."
- "Wouldn't it be wonderful?"
- "It would be great if..."

and, of course, "wouldn't it be nice' are all workable versions, or you can create your own. Just use words that speak to you of being playful and open to wonderful possibilities.

I'd also recommend that, once you have your phrase, you use the same one every time. Consistency tends to build energy in these things, and also makes them easier to do.

Once you have your phrase, put it with your statement. Say it out loud, paying attention to how you feel while you do it.

Note any signs of resistance?

If yes, you may need to soften the statement further. (For instance, when using our example above, "wouldn't it be nice if my body were always strong and healthy?" could still be powerful enough to trigger resistance, but "wouldn't it be nice if my body were strong and healthy most of the time?" might be softened enough to completely sidestep any resistance.

If you have no signs of resistance, you now have a personalized "wouldn't it be nice…" statement that's ready to start working with.

You have your starting statement, but you're not necessarily going to stop there. Many techniques, such as affirmations work with repeating the same statement over and over, but in this process, the statements can expand and build on each other.

You can just make one "wouldn't it be nice." statement and leave it there, or you and your manifestation buddy can bounce that statement back and forth. For instance:

- "Wouldn't it be nice if it was sunny this afternoon so we could go to the park?"
- "Yes, that would be nice if it was sunny and we could go have fun in the park.

but you can also use that base statement as a

springboard to bigger and bigger manifestations. To work with the "wouldn't it be nice" process, you don't always just keep with the one statement. For instance:

- "Wouldn't it be nice if it was sunny this afternoon so we could go to the park?"
- "Yes, that would be great if it was sunny and we could go have fun in the park; and wouldn't it be nice if we met some interesting new people while we were there?"
- "That would be wonderful, and wouldn't it be nice if those people knew about an event where we could get our new music group out in front of the public?"
- "I'd love that, and wouldn't it be great if they could get us in for free?"

And so forth. This is one of the advantages of playing with this with two or more people, because with people who are positive, enthusiastic and enjoying this, you can build to bigger and more beautiful things.

Interestingly enough, when you either go back and forth like this, or build a sequence of statements like this on your own, some statements that might have originally triggered resistance if you'd started with them, completely bypass resistance if you dance up to them like we did in the example. It's a funny phenomenon, worth knowing.

I realize that the previous section makes it sound like this is a solemn and serious process, which requires a great deal of preparation.

It isn't really. I want to show you the steps of how it comes together, but once you've played with it a bit, you'll be able to easily do this on the fly, with no preparation whatsoever.

And I do use the word "play" intentionally. When this process is at its best, it's fun and playful and easy. I often find myself getting a funny little grin on my face while I do it, because it is so fun and playful a way to make good and amazing things happen.

Enjoy the process. Value it. But don't take it too seriously. It works best if you do it in a spirit of fun.

The "wouldn't it be nice" technique is generally useful because it's flexible, low-key and less likely to trigger resistance, but even it has some limits. It's possible to over-reach yourself enough to stretch even this method until you hit some resistance.

As one example:

"A few months back, my husband Starwolf and I were camping out at a renaissance faire. We had just climbed into bed in our booth when rain began to patter on the roof of the tent.

We looked at each other. Rain could mean no customers the following day, and, on top of that, meant packing up wet gear for a long drive back home at the end of the weekend. No fun that.

So we started to play the gentle manifestation game called "wouldn't it be nice?"...

"Wouldn't it be nice" I said "if the rain eased off..."

And, interestingly enough, the rain slowed a bit...

"Wouldn't it be nice" said Starwolf "if the rain turned to a slight drizzle and nothing more...?"

And the rain slowed even more...

> *"Wouldn't it be nice"* I said *"if it stopped raining altogether...?"*
>
> *And the rain totally stopped.*
>
> *In the darkness, Starwolf looked at me. I looked back at him.*
>
> *"Wouldn't it be nice"* said Starwolf *"if we won several million dollars in the lottery..."*
>
> *And the rain began to fall again. Hard..."*

So what happened with that?

Well, in theory, it's no more difficult to manifest a million dollars than a cup of coffee. In practice, however, our beliefs on what is possible and how hard it is to obtain something have a significant effect on how effective we are at manifestation. When we believe that it's harder to manifest one thing than another, or that manifestation doesn't work at all, we create resistance, which can make it harder to manifest something.

Because weather fluctuates, we may believe it's easier to take something that changes a lot anyway and just "give it a nudge" in the direction we want. For that reason, many people find it easier to believe that weather can be nudged or influenced than it is to believe we can create something (like a lottery win) out of nothing.

When we believe that weather can possibly be more easily influenced, a gentle manifestation technique (like "wouldn't it be nice...?") works well on it. Because it's a bigger leap of faith to believe that one can manifest a financial windfall of that level, it's harder to jumpstart a manifestation of that sort (and the rain restarted just so the Universe could make that point...)

When it comes to beliefs, people are funny about money. (That includes me.) More of us have blockages and resistance about manifesting money than almost any other topic. For this reason, while manifesting money is definitely possible, it's more likely to trigger resistance than most other topics. That means that, depending on what your personal beliefs or blockages are, you may have to go more slowly or take baby steps to get around that resistance.

Remember when I was talking about paying attention for signs of resistance? Well, in this case, we got a strong external sign from the elements, and that's a signal that we needed to slow up, soften the statement and try again….

You make your statement.

You make as many statements as feel right to you.

You watch for resistance and modify or soften your statements as needed

And then you watch for the results.

That's all there is to the "wouldn't it be nice…" technique, a very simple, playful, fun way of changing the Universe…..

Chapter 16
Setting An Intention

One morning, I set an intention for a day filled with delightful surprises.

Later, at the local health food store, the woman who waited on me started a wonderful conversation out of the blue. She also gave me a gourmet chocolate. (This was not a sample situation and had never happened before.)

At my next stop, I found a new book by a favorite writer (a book that I hadn't heard of.)

And at the stop after that, I came around a corner and came across an old friend I hadn't seen for years.

Interesting...

In chapter 3, we talked about intentions as metaphysical goals, and how "setting an intention" is the metaphysical way of creating a target or goal to focus the energy you're working with. What we didn't say is that simply setting an intention can be an effective method of creating a better reality for ourselves. We've been setting an intention to target something specific. We can also do this in a more open, less specific manner, inviting a more general type of experience into our lives and leaving the Universe lots of wiggle room in how to make that happen.

Let's set an intention for this chapter to be particularly useful to you, and look at this way of using the power of intention.

The basic process of this kind of setting an intention is deceptively simple. You start with a phrase such as "It is my intention that..." and then you add on a positive statement. It can be a more specific statement, such as:

- …I finish writing a minimum of three more chapters on my first draft today.
- …I impress the management in my interview and am called back for a second interview for this job.
- …the package I am waiting for arrives today in the mail.

It can also be a more general statement, such as

- ….today is a day of delightful surprises.
- …today I receive good news all day.
- ….today is a day where I accomplish everything on my to-do list easily, joyously, and with style and panache.

Then stand back and watch what happens.

Simple, right? It almost seems too simple; but it's really surprising how effective this simple little method can be for unknotting problems, making amazing things happen, and improving the overall quality of your life.

How does this work? The core of this deceptively simple process is the statement "It is my intention that…"

For many processes, you ask for something by making a clear cut and concrete statement

- My package arrives today.

That statement's fine, but tends to trigger resistance, and the bigger the shift you're trying to do, the more resistance you'll be fighting upstream against.

Now try this instead:

- It is my intention that my package arrives today.

When, on the other hand, you use a phrase like "It is my intention that..." you soften the energy of the statement. You're not insisting that it must be so. It's just something you intend; something that you're working towards. Those dragons of resistance we talked about before don't even wake up.

Now, I've found that particular wording very useful, but you don't have to follow the words exactly, as long as you have a phrase that catches its meaning. Phrases such as:

- I'd like it if…
- I'm looking forwards to a day where…
- I'm anticipating…

…all would work, or you can find one that works for you. Chose words that indicate positive anticipation without forcing the issue and you have what you need.

Then use it, and use it often. The Universe has no limits on how often you can ask for good things, so it's a good thing to get in the habit of doing so with frequency and joy.

There are things that you can do to strengthen your intention statements and make them more effective without triggering resistance.

The first is to use positive statements. Don't use words like "no" or "not" in manifestation work if you can avoid it. For some reason, the unconscious mind, which holds the mind-body connection and a lot of the power of manifestation, doesn't hear these negative words, and that can really mess up what you manifest. For instance, if you say

- I have no pain.

Your unconscious hears this as "I have pain." and does its best to make this happen. Instead, you want to use a positive phrase like:

- I am free of pain.
  or
- I feel great!

to avoid fighting yourself.

Next, what you want to do is to use juicy words or phrases.

- It is my intention that today is a wonderful day full of excellent news and delightful events

has far more power than

- It is my intention that today goes ok.

And it's the kind of power that increases powerful results without tripping resistance. Use words and phrases like "delightful", "fun", "wonderful", and "amazingly simple" to power up your intentions.

Finally, develop a list of favorite words, phrases and requests, and use them often. The more you use them, the easier it will become to use them, and there's no limit on how much joy you can have in your life.

Once you set your intention, take time to watch what happens, especially if you've asked for one of the more general, open ended ones.

This technique is amazingly effective, and can bring good things into your life in surprising ways. Many times, how it works not only fills me with delight, but has actually given me the giggles because it's so charming, unexpected and fun.

Pay attention for the entertainment value, but also for another reason. Because this is a subtle technique, the results are often subtle themselves, or things our minds will explain away if we don't consciously pay attention. That's ok, but if we watch and see that it works, this increases our belief in the technique which improves how well it works. That's worth doing.

Set your intention and watch for results. You'll surprise yourself.

As I said before, this is a no limits technique. It's

short, quick and easy to do; you can do it as often as you like; and there are no limits to how much joy you can have in your life. For this reason, this is a technique you can and should use often; but oddly enough, even people who know it and how well it works have a tendency to forget to use it. That's a pity, especially when it can make your life so much better in so many ways.

This technique can be used on the fly whenever it seems appropriate and useful, such as

- It is my intention that, when I get to the store, I'll find an open parking spot I'm entitled to use near to the entrance I want to use.

But I'd also recommend that you build in specific times during your day to do quality of life intentions. Doing it in the morning before you get out of bed is one option, at night for the following day is another or at any other point in your routine that works for you.

Building a habit of intention will mean you'll use it, not forget it; and pairing it with other things you do every day helps you build that manifestation routine.

Quick. Easy. Fun. Effective. That's setting an intention – the little process that can move mountains. Now that you know how to do it and how it works, it's time for you to set some intentions of your own.

Have fun with this, and when you're ready, come back for the next process.

Chapter 17
The "Previewing" Technique

So far, we've looked at two different methods using words alone to ask for what we're trying to manifest. Now it's time to use all of our senses.

The next process is called previewing. Previewing is a process where you use visualizations to set the scene for the life you want to have. Despite its name, visualization doesn't just involve vision. In this case, visualization means making a mental picture of what you want to happen, using input from as many senses as possible.

In previewing, we picture your life as a movie. In movies, the story is broken down into scenes. Each scene is located in a different place or contains a specific activity. When doing this process, we're going to break your life down in the same way, and you get to be the director in the movie of your life.

Think of your life as a movie. Getting up in the morning and getting ready for your day is a scene. Driving to work is a scene. A team meeting or the workday from the time you get in until lunch can be a scene. You break your life into scenes based on naturally occurring landmarks, when you move from one activity to another.

Try it now. What are some of the scenes that you've experienced in the past two days?

Once you've got the hang of seeing things as scenes, you're ready to preview.

As you move through your actual day in your life, take a minute to stop just before entering each scene. Close your eyes for a minute if possible, and picture the next scene how you would like it to go:

- Easy meeting, with people co-operating with each other?
- Smooth morning shift with everyone working well together?
- Great commute, missing traffic and stops?

(If it's not possible to close your eyes, then, in your head, run over a list of what you'd like to happen.)

Picture it as you'd like it to go, and then open your eyes and move forwards into the scene that you have already laid the groundwork for.

And watch what happens…

Let's take a closer look at visualization for the process of previewing. There are several components you need to include in these visualizations.

First, be as specific as you need to be, and no more so. Make your picture as vivid as possible, but only picture details that are important to you, leaving room for the Universe to meet your request in ways you hadn't thought of.

Next, you need to bring as many of your senses into the visualizations as possible. Don't just see a new red sports car. Hear the sound of its' motor roaring. Feel the softness of the leather seat covers and the sensation of acceleration. Smell that new car smell.

Third, put yourself in the picture. Don't just picture

that car- picture yourself in that car and enjoying it.

And finally, when in doubt, feel the emotion. If you know you want a positive result in a situation, but you're open to different ways that can happen or you're not sure what a positive resolution would be, focus on the emotions you want to feel. Picture yourself cheering, fist pumping or grinning like an idiot. Just like any other visualization, make this image as vivid as possible, including how your body feels with this emotion.

Make sure to include these components to get the best effect from previewing.

Should you do big scenes or small ones? Do you have to preview every scene in every single part of your day? Those are two more worthwhile questions.

My impression is that previewing generally works best in small scenes. It's easier to make a richer, more complete visualization if you're only covering a short time, rather than an entire week at once. If, however, your life makes it hard to visualize throughout your day, it's workable to visualize a successful day in one sitting.

As for how much of your day you need to preview, I'd say as much as you want to. There will be times when you'll feel a scene will go just fine and doesn't need any metaphysical help from you.

Be sure not to sell this method short though. It can be useful for small things as well as big ones. Keep it in mind for traffic jams, parking spaces and getting that callback you've been waiting for, as well as changing reality in bigger ways.

Previewing is a process that can and should be done on an ongoing basis. Every time you visualize, you make your reality a little bit better, <u>and</u>, on top of that, you get a little bit better at visualizing. For those reasons, if you choose to preview, you should do it regularly and you should do it often. That being said, it's good to have a routine for previewing.

You can choose to have regular times of day when you preview:

- In the morning, preview a great day before you get out of bed.
- In the parking lot, preview a smooth day at work before you go into your workplace.
- At lunch, preview an easy afternoon when everything comes together easily and joyously.
- Before you drive home, preview a good commute with no traffic.
- At night, as you fall asleep, preview a great day tomorrow.

You can also use situational cues to remind you to preview.

- When you brush your teeth.
- When you get in or out of the car.
- At mealtimes, or
- When you see a card that says "Preview" taped to places you frequently look, such as in your day

planner, on your dashboard or next to your bathroom mirror

Build yourself a routine for previewing, and find ways to remind yourself to do it regularly.

Whether you're working on big things or on little ones, previewing is a great way to ask for what you want and work with energy to attain it. Start playing with it now, and see how the power of your mind can affect the world around you.

And now let's move on to the next step of the manifestation process – receiving.

Receive

Chapter 18
On Receiving

We've tweaked and adjusted our energy to be as positive as possible. We've figured out what we really wanted and we've asked for it.

And, if we've tweaked and energized and asked well, what we want is on the way.

Here comes the fun part. Receiving.

This section has processes to prepare to receive what we've asked for, and opening a space to receive our new reality into our lives. There are things you can do to make receiving easier and more efficient. We've got some good ones here for you.

Get ready for fun. Get ready for the universe to change...

Chapter 19
The "Act as If" Technique

You've placed your request and the people, things, or situations you've requested are making their way through the cosmos in your direction. What can you do to help them arrive faster and to prevent resistance from cropping up and interfering with things?

You can do a process called "Act as if".

The simplest description of this process is that, when you're setting a goal or intention, you figure out how you'd behave if your intention was already reality. Then, you act that way. Changing your behavior sends a message to your unconscious that things are different- that your intention is already reality. Getting that message, your unconscious mind will then put all of its resources behind bringing actual reality into line with that concept.

The "Act as if" process can be applied in lots of ways in manifestation. In this case, we're going to use it for seeing the intention we're manifesting as already here.

When you order a sofa from a mail order business and arrange to have it delivered, you don't call them back every five minutes, saying "Are you re…ally going to deliver a sofa to me?"

Nope. You place your order, and then you start moving the rest of your furniture to make room for the new couch. You don't worry or fret about whether it's coming or not. You don't ask yourself "But what if they never bring it?" You know that it's coming. You've done what you needed to do to get a couch delivered and, while there may be a bit of uncertainty about delivery windows, you're sure in the knowledge that your sofa is on its way.

As it is in retail, so should it be in manifestation work. When you work with energy to manifest something, cultivate a feeling of surety of the results in yourself. Don't "what if" yourself into doubt or anxiety. Feel certain and prepare for things to happen.

What are some things that you can do to "act as if" and prepare for your intention to arrive?

- If you're manifesting a better place to live, you can start weeding out belongings you won't want to move and packing off season clothing.
- If you're manifesting a better job, you can review your work wardrobe for what would be suitable for your new position, and fill in gaps in your attire.
- If you're manifesting someone special to love in your life, you can clean out closet space for them and start sleeping on one side of the bed.

There's lots of thing that you can do to signal to the Universe that you know your intention is on its way.

One caution with this technique- it's helpful to "Act as if" but it's best to do it with the resources that you currently have to work with. Since changing reality means shifting things around in the universe, it doesn't always come together at the exact time we're expecting. At that point, it's powerful to know things are coming, but it's good not to rely on them arriving in our lives on a set schedule.

When I was a child, there was a special feeling we used to get around Christmas time. It was an almost overwhelming feeling of "I'm not sure exactly what's going to happen, but I know that it's gonna be AMAZING!!!" The kind of feeling where you almost need to hug yourself because you're so excited.

Not everyone is Christian, celebrates Christmas or has had that kind of holiday experience; but I'd like to share my Christmas morning feeling with you all because it's very useful to everyone who's doing manifestation. That feeling of intense anticipation, of uncertainty of how but surety of delight, of joy almost bigger than you can contain is a beacon to the Universe that draws your manifestation in. It boosts your positive energy a thousand fold and increases your power of attraction to the things you want.

If you haven't had a feeling like this as a holiday experience, then I'd urge you to search your memory for something that's given you that feeling of expectation and delight, and use the memory of that feeling to power your present manifestations. If you can't put your finger on a time you've felt like that before, I make you a gift of my own remembered feeling. Borrow the description and try to feel what it would be like to feel like that.

Once you've started your manifestation work, once you've asked and are entering the period of receiving, do your best to try and experience feelings like this one. They feel great and they make your work more powerful.

For a stronger experience of "Act as If", you can visualize what it will be like when what you are manifesting has arrived.

Close your eyes. Build up a picture in your head of what it will feel like. Make it as vivid as possible. Just as we did in the process for previewing:

- Be as specific as you need and no more so,
- Involve as many of your senses in the visualization as possible,
- Put yourself in the picture and
- Include the emotions you'll feel as part of the experience.

Take the time you need to really get into the experience and enjoy it. If you find yourself grinning, you're doing it right. Do it often, because every time you do it, you're sending a message to the Universe that this is what you want.

And have fun with it. The good feelings you have doing this now are a preview of what's coming in your future.

When we "Act as if", we put the power of our energy and our unconscious mind squarely in the service of the manifestation that is in process. We shape reality with our behavior and bring it into alignment with our dreams.

Try "Acting as if" and see what it can help you create.

Chapter 20
Paying Attention to Signs from the Universe

I had hit a point when I was stuck while writing this book. A point I was trying to make just wouldn't gel, no matter which direction I come from. I consulted the I Ching (a Chinese method divination) and was told that I needed to stop and take a brief rest before my writing would flow freely again.

Ugh. Waiting. One of my less favorite things- but I wasn't getting anywhere the way I was going.

So I took a break...

And I must admit that, after that hiatus, my energy felt better. Words began to flow freely again and the point that was so difficult just fell together in no time.

You've prepared your energy and asked for what you want. Now it's time for things to start happening.

Sometimes a manifestation is absolutely blatant. You try to manifest a car and you get a phone call saying you've won a sedan in a drawing you entered last week.

Sometimes the results are more subtle.

When you do manifestation work, sometimes what you've requested arrives directly without any further steps; but sometimes you get cues, omens, or signs that will lead you to your intention instead. Because of this, when you're doing manifestation, it's important to stay alert and to listen to what messages the Universe is sending you about your intention.

Let's look at different things we can do to listen to the Universe and be aware of the messages it's sending to us.

When you start out with manifestation, one thing you'll find is that you'll be getting messages in ways you're not used to. You may get vague impressions or impulses to do something. Your body may tell you things too. It can feel weird or strange, and one of your first impulses will be to talk yourself out of it.

- When I think about this choice, I feel sick to my stomach. I guess lunch disagrees with me.
- I don't know why, but I feel like I should go to this event; though I had other plans and there's no logical reason for me to go.
- This is a perfectly respectable person, and there's no reason that I should feel nervous about him.

All three of these statements are ways that the Universe is trying to move you closer to what you're trying to manifest or further away from what you're not, but because they're not coming in the logic based formats we're used to, we've learned to second guess ourselves.

I'm not saying to turn off your brains. (I would never want anyone to do that.) I am saying, however, that you should keep in mind that you have other ways of receiving information than you're used to, and you need to take all kinds of input in mind and weigh each piece for its' own value when you're manifesting.

One source of information during manifestation is

feedback from your body.

Do you remember how we looked at messages from your body earlier in this book when we talked about resistance? That was useful, and your body can give you much more information that can help with manifestation.

- It can tell you when you're going the wrong way (ex: hesitation, nausea, or stiffness)
- It can tell you if you're heading into dangerous territory (Ex: hair rising on the back of your neck or feeling hyper-alert)
- It can tell you if there's somewhere you need to go or something you need to do. (Ex: feeling relaxed but alert and curious when you think about an option.)
- It can tell you when you're on the right track (Ex: feeling relaxed, comfortable and happy.)

In metaphysics, many times our intuition picks up on things we're not consciously aware of, and sends us messages through our bodies, because those signals are more concrete and easily perceived.

There are lots of different reasons why your body can have one or more of these sensations, but if you're doing manifestation and you suddenly feel nervous and hyper-alert, or your body relaxes and feels strong and flexible, it's worth thinking about whether your unconscious mind could be sending you messages about your manifestation through your body.

Sometimes manifestation is a car pulling up in the driveway and the driver handing us the keys. Sometimes, though, it arrives as openings and opportunities to reach what we're manifesting.

Perhaps you're trying to manifest a year in France. You do the work, and when you look in the paper, there's suddenly a program for an academic fellowship in France with all expenses paid. All you have to do is get the forms and fill them out.

Perfect.

Now part of that process was watching and listening for the opening that you knew was coming because you'd done the work. That one was fairly straight forward, but sometimes they're more obscure. When doing manifestation work, you'll want to watch for things that keep popping up repeatedly in your life that weren't frequent before. If you want that trip to France, and suddenly you keep seeing the same French car everywhere you go, you might want to check into it. Maybe they have a contest for a year in France running (or are about to run one…) If you find the same person's name keeps cropping up around you, you might want to check into him more or contact him if you can. Maybe he needs a caretaker for his cottage in France for the next year.

Watch for those frequent encounters or "co-incidences" as they may be signposts to where you need to be going. Watch too for opportunities or openings that may lead to what you're trying to manifest.

We've listened to our bodies. We've watched for

openings and co-incidences. Now, taking it one step further, we need to listen to our own inner wisdom- that little voice inside of us.

Sometimes, you'll just get a feeling that you should do something. Turn left not right. Take a different route home from the grocery store. Go to a talk you weren't planning on going to. Most of the time, a majority of us talk ourselves out of these little hunches.

When you're doing manifestation work, it's important to at least listen to that little voice and follow it where possible. You may not always be able to drop everything, but it's good to listen, and do what you can. This is another way our intuition can be guiding us to the reality we're trying to manifest, so it makes sense to take it seriously.

These instincts may not always make sense at first – but many times, they will lead us to something important and we'll have the "a ha!" moment where it all makes sense.

These instincts are not always about the manifestation work either. Our inner voice speaks to us on quite a number of assorted topics, including manifestation, so a message may actually be in regard to something else important in our lives. At that point, it's still good to listen.

You just need to remember to trust your intuition, because it's another method the Universes uses to guide you to your dreams.

Besides our bodies, openings and opportunities, and our inner wisdom, what are some other ways the Universe tries to give us information?

- Dreams.
- Increased frequency. If, all of a sudden, you're seeing pregnant women, or red sports cars, or references to Hawaii far more often than you did previously, the Universe may be trying to tell you something.
- Random comments.
- Songs on the radio or shows on TV. What jumps out at you when you channel surf?
- Networking, where someone you meet casually has the missing piece of information you're looking for or knows someone who can ask.
- And a wide range of other so-called "co-incidences".

There's lots of ways the Universe can try to reach us. We just need to be alert and listen for it.

Whether it's input from our bodies or our intuition or the hand of "co-incidence", when we start the work of manifestation, we will receive guidance as we go on how we can change our reality for the better.

All we need to do is to listen for that guidance…

…And act on it. And that's in the next chapter…

Chapter 21
Now, Take Inspired Action

In the last chapter, we talked about listening to messages from the Universe that lead to the manifestation of our dreams. This chapter's about the step that follows that – about taking inspired action in response to the information we've been sent.

As I said before, sometimes the Universe parks a new car in your driveway- and sometimes it sends a notice of where you need to go to pick it up. We talked in the last chapter about paying attention and listening to messages the Universe is sends us about what we are manifesting. Sometimes listening is enough to get us where we need to go; but often we need to listen and then take inspired action. Inspired action is what you do based on these messages you're getting from the Universe.

- Looking in a paper you usually don't read and finding the listing for the perfect job.
- Putting an entry into a contest.
- Applying to a school that you didn't think you could get into because something tells you to apply.

Inspired action is giving your instincts legs and walking them in the direction of your dreams.

At this point, some of you may be saying "Well,

where's the manifestation in all of that? I could have just applied to college or for the job, and skipped all of the energy work." To make this clearer, there are two big differences between simple action and inspired action.

The first difference is the inspiration itself. This isn't just doing something because you want to, or because it seems like the right thing to do, or because it "makes sense", or because "why not?" This is applying energy towards manifesting your dreams, and getting back information that helps you sort out the action most likely to succeed from all of the hundreds of other possible "right things to do." Wouldn't a clear sign in life that said "For best effect, apply effort here" be useful? Inspiration makes a real difference in what you do and saves you lots of wasted effort and heartbreak. Manifestation work is one way to access that inspiration.

The second difference involves the amount of action needed. Often, manifestation work draws what you ask for into your life with no further effort on your part. Sometimes though, there seems to be a need for a limited amount of action on your part. To illustrate:

"There was a man named John who everyday prayed to God "Dear God, please let me win the lottery today."

And John never won.

Many years later, he died and went to Heaven, and when he met God, he put his hands on his hips and said "God, I prayed to you daily for over 50 years for you to let me win the lottery, and I never did. Why didn't you ever grant me what I prayed for?"

And God looked down at him and said gently "John, would it have hurt you to buy a ticket..?"

Some manifestations seem to require a certain amount of effort from us on the physical plane. It's almost as if that action is a measure of our commitment to what we're manifesting, and once we take that action, things start to move for us.

When inspired action is needed for a particular manifestation, I find that the actual action need is usually far less than it would be if I were going for the same thing without energy work. Things go more smoothly, pleasant "co-incidences" just "pop up", and things fall in to place in surprising ways.

It's worth doing the inspired action and letting the Universe do the majority of the work for me.

How do we tell the difference between inspiration and a plain old ordinary everyday impulse? Most inspiration comes to us as feelings or hunches that at first may not make any subjective sense.

- A feeling that you should take a different route home from work.
- Being drawn to a job listing in a newspaper.
- Finding yourself fascinated by someone you've just met at a party, who turns out to be the brother of

someone you end up dating.

There are impulses as a part of inspiration, but they're a special kind of impulse. They're a feeling that we just "should do" a particular thing without any rhyme or reason to it.

Two key factors are that, 1) while inspiration can often have a feeling of urgency to it, at the core the feeling is usually calm and clear; and 2) the information that comes to us does not always make sense at first, but it "feels right."

More mundane impulses, on the other hand, are usually quite understandable. We get an impulse for a hot fudge sundae, or a shopping spree, or to ignore that work project in favor of something more fun, and we have no questions whatsoever about where these impulses came from.

Regular impulses are fine in moderation, but it's important not to confuse them with inspiration.

Sometimes, your inspiration won't make sense to you at first. When that happens, your options are to:

- Follow it anyway, and see what happens; or
- Walk away.

The choice is yours.

Many times, I've found that following that cue even though I didn't know why has made things open up for me in a delightful and surprising way.

It's worth noting though that you don't necessarily only get one chance. If you choose to walk away from one option because it seems questionable, you'll often find that another option comes along later if you keep doing the manifestation work.

Now, in the course of using your inspiration, you want to use your logic as well. Don't turn off your brain and do something stupid. Rather, it's important to trust your inspiration but bring your logic into things as a backup safety check. For instance:

- *Inspiration* I've been doing manifestation work to find love, and I'm getting a feeling I should attend a presentation that's being offered downtown tonight
- *Logic* Is there anything more important I need to do that I can't do at another time? *No*
- *Logic* Can I afford it? *Yes*
- *Logic* Is there any reason not to go downtown? *No*
- *Inspiration and Logic Together* Then let's go!

Don't turn off your brain. Don't ignore your intuition. They're both there for a reason, and you need to teach them to work together to get the best results.

Don't do dumb things, but do take inspired action, and let the Universe meet you most of the way.

Sometimes in manifestation work, all we need to do

is ask, but sometimes we need to take inspired action to make a commitment to what we're trying to manifest.

Be sure to listen to the Universe as you work with energy, and take inspired action on the way to the reality you're looking for.

Multi-Purpose

Chapter 22
On Multipurpose Techniques

We've gone through processes for preparing our energy, for asking for what we want, and for receiving the good things that we choose to manifest. Sometimes, though, a process is good for more than one step, and doesn't fit neatly into one category or another.

That's what this section holds- the Swiss army knives of simple manifestation, the metaphysical workhorses of changing reality. Welcome to the section of processes good for more than one manifestation step - the one-man bands of energy work. By using these processes, you can work a choice of steps or can work more than one step at a time, doing double or triple duty in a pinch.

When you're looking for the right process for something you're working on, don't forget to check this section. What you need may be right here.

Chapter 23
Using Affirmations
(Preparing Your Energy/Asking)

We've arrived in the section of processes good for more than one step in manifestation, and we're going to start with a classic in self-improvement <u>and</u> metaphysics. Let's begin with affirmations, a process good for both preparing your energy field and asking for what you want.

What is an affirmation, anyway? An affirmation is a positive statement repeated multiple times to reprogram the unconscious mind by clearing out dysfunctional beliefs and replacing them with more useful ones.

Since we know that our beliefs tend to create our emotions and determine the energy we put out, and that shapes the nature of reality around us, having a tool that lets us choose what beliefs we hold is useful.

Let's look at those beliefs a bit more.

We all have beliefs we've picked up throughout our lives. Some of them serve us well (Ex: I can succeed if I put my mind to it), some of them worked for a time, but are no longer useful, (Ex: Don't cross the street unless you're holding a grown-up's hand), and some have never been helpful. (Ex: You're a loser and you'll always be a loser).

Positive beliefs come from all kinds of places. Some are things we are taught, and some are things we learn from experience. Dysfunctional beliefs come from the exact same places, and it's worth knowing that negative beliefs can be taught to us by people who love us and are trying to protect us, (Ex: You can't make a living doing art.) or learned by taking the wrong lesson away from an experience. (Ex: He broke my heart. All men are pigs!)

In any case, the best option we have is looking at our own beliefs, deciding for ourselves which ones are working for us and which ones aren't, and releasing the ones that don't work.

Affirmations let us do this.

Most of the beliefs we've learned through life are learned through repetition. If you're told everyday for twenty one years that "you're the smart one, not the pretty one," you accept that belief and that's the reality you manifest.

Affirmations work on the same principle. It took lots of repetition to put that dysfunctional belief in place, and it's going to take a lot of repetition to program a new, more helpful belief and to shoot the old belief out of your head in the process. Experts in the field say that it takes 1000 repetitions of an affirmation to find it a permanent home in your unconscious mind. I've found that 1000 reps is good to make sure that you've locked that belief in, but the odds are good that you'll start seeing positive results long before that.

Repeating something one thousand times sounds like a lot, but if it only takes a couple of seconds per rep, that's not a long time, especially when you compare it to the amount of time in your life that is improved because you do this in the first place.

There are lots of affirmations already out there that you can choose to use, (Ex: Every day in every way, I am getting better and better.) and I'd urge you to use any one of these that speaks to you, but I find many times that the most useful affirmations are the ones we create ourselves for our own unique needs.

How do you create an affirmation? What are the pieces you need to include in one?

The basic pieces of an affirmation are this:

- They're better if they're short. (Ex: I am healthy.)
- They're easy to say. (Ex: I'm strong and healthy in body, mind and spirit.)
- They're phrased in the present tense, as if what you want has already happened. (Ex:"I have a job I love" as opposed to "I will have a job I love.")
- They use positive words and phrases. (Ex: "I have all the money I want." not "I am not poor.")
- They're better when they use "juicy" words that are full of energy. (Ex: "My life is exciting and delightful." as opposed to "My life is good.")
- You put yourself in them. (Ex: "I live in a wonderful world." not "This is a wonderful world.")
- They work better when said with emotion as opposed to being repeated in a monotone.

Let's look at those points more closely.

<u>They're better if they're short</u>. A short affirmation is easier to focus on and easier to say, especially in quantity.

<u>They're easy to say.</u> If you verbally stumble over them, you'll lose your focus. Say them out loud to test them before you use them

<u>They're phrased in the present tense, as if what you want has already happened.</u> If you use words like "will" that put what you want in the future, you manifest your goal coming in a future that never arrives.

<u>They use positive words and phrases.</u> Your unconscious doesn't hear words like "no" and "not", so if you affirm "I am not sick", you manifest "I am sick." Instead, use positive words like "I am well."

<u>They're better when they use "juicy" words that are full of energy.</u> Words that are colorful and exciting channel more energy than words that are half-hearted or "blah". Choose words that make the affirmation more exciting.

<u>You put yourself in them…</u> or else you manifest something that doesn't involve you.

<u>They work better when said with emotion as opposed to just repeated in a monotone.</u> Since we know that emotion helps set the level of our energetic field, it's not hard to see that saying something in an enthusiastic way brings more energy to bear on the manifestation process.

All of these points are suggestions not rigid rules, and a good affirmation may not use all of them. If you feel guided to ignore one or more of these, please do, but keep them in mind as good guidelines for creating an effective affirmation. The important point is developing the affirmation that best meets your personal needs.

Once you've created your affirmation, it's time to work with it. There's a number of good ways to do that. Keep in mind that you need to repeat an affirmation 1000 times for it to stick in your unconscious, though you may start to see its influence long before that many repetitions.

The first and most frequently used way to work with affirmations is to say them out loud. You don't have to say them 1000 times all at once though. Indeed, I'd advise against it. Saying something 1000 times in a row at one sitting is tedious, and tedium can rob your affirmation of its energy. It's much easier to stay enthusiastic in small bursts or affirmation sprints.

You can break your 1000 affirmations into smaller groups, which are easier to fit in throughout the day. At a red light. When you're alone in an elevator. When you're washing your hands. There are lots of times in your routine where you can say some affirmations if you have privacy.

I like to break them down into groups of ten. With the type of affirmations I usually use, I find a group of ten usually takes between ten and thirty seconds, a convenient size to fit into many parts of my day. Broken into groups of ten, I only need to do a group 100 times, and that's pretty workable.

If you're going to break your affirmations into groups, you'll need a way to keep track of how many groups you've done. I have a page in my Day Runner with the affirmation listed and space below to mark with each group of ten. You may like to do it this way, or you may choose another.

Saying affirmations isn't the only way to work with them. You can also write them 1000 times. Remember those old school teachers who had kids write "I will not talk in class." repeatedly on the board? They had something going there, because writing your affirmation over and over can also help to change your unconscious beliefs.

Whether you're saying or writing, remember to put as much emotion into it as you can. If you're saying your affirmation, say it with enthusiasm. If you're writing it, try to feel good about what you're writing. In either case, smile while you affirm and feel the joy of anticipation. Your affirmations help your intention to come into your life.

So that's the basics of affirmations, a powerful tool for manifestation. Affirmations are good for increasing your positive energy. They're good for asking the Universe for what you want. But most of all, affirmations are good for changing your mind, and better beliefs mean manifesting better things in your life.

Chapter 24
Working with Gratitude
(Preparing Your Energy/ Receiving)

I had missed the deadline...

My dad's eightieth birthday was fast approaching. I'd been working overtime to finish my first fantasy novel as a birthday gift dedicated to him. He had introduced me to fantasy stories when I was young and had always supported my writing, so I felt my first novel would be something he'd like.

Unfortunately, Life happens, especially when time grows short. I'd not only missed my deadline, but was a week behind when I finally sent my manuscript in.

Three to five days to complete a printed book. Two day express shipping, for a total of five to seven days, if all went well. And I'd sent it in at 4 p.m. on Monday afternoon, needing it by Friday for the Saturday celebration.

The math said this wasn't gonna happen.

I was sad at first, but then I started to think about what was good here. The book was finished, and I was pleased with the story. I was blessed to have a father who loved me and who supported my dreams. I was fortunate to be able to celebrate his eightieth birthday with him. I knew that, even if all I could give him for now was a copy of the cover and a promise, he'd be proud of me and love the present.

I counted my blessings and was grateful for them.

And slightly over twenty six hours later (as opposed to three to five days), I received an email notifying me that my book was complete and on the way...

Having looked at affirmations for preparing our energy and asking for what we want, let's move on to another way of improving our energy and also for receiving. Let's look at gratitude work.

Gratitude work is the process of appreciating what's already right in our world. Just as affirmations were good both for improving our energy and for asking the Universe for what we want, gratitude work is good for raising our energetic level and for making receiving easier, quicker and smoother. It can help with decreasing resistance, and it feels good, too….

So how does gratitude help with manifestation?

Your mother was right, you know. If your mother was like mine, there were times in your life when she told you to be thankful for what you had or to count your blessings. Energetically, that's one of the smartest things you could do.

As we already know, what we put most of our attention on tends to determine what we attract or manifest into our lives. Focus on what's good about your life and you tend to draw more good things. Focus on what's bad or lacking and draw more bad things or lack of good.

Furthermore, we not only draw more of what we focus on, but also other things that make us feel the same way. In other words, if you like hot fudge sundaes and think about them a lot, you'll not only draw more hot fudge sundaes into your life but also triple fudge milkshakes (and perhaps someone nice to share them with…)

This doesn't just work on things like ice cream. Big or small, it works for all, and the positive energy that starts with saying blessings for your meal or appreciating a comfortable pair of shoes can spiral upwards to bigger examples of happiness and prosperity.

The basic premise of "like calls to like" is a good enough reason by itself to practice gratitude, but there's more to it than that. Gratitude work can also help us overcome some kinds of resistance. Certain kinds of resistance are based in the question of "worthiness":

- "I'm not worthy to have so much good in my life"
- "Other people deserve this more than I do."

Counting our blessings and feeling gratitude helps us be more aware of all the good already in our lives; and provides evidence that we're worthy of joy and blessings.

Counting your blessings and feeling gratitude for what you already have is a great way to bring even better things into your life.

So, how do we do gratitude work?

One way is by sharing the wealth, as we spoke of in chapter 13, but there's lots of other different ways to do it. For instance:

- **Say thank you.** Simple, right? But noticing how others help you and thanking them brings gratitude into your life as a regular spiritual practice.
- **Call the manager.** When you get good service, call and praise as opposed to complain. Great for your energy and makes someone else's day as well.
- **Make a "my favorite things" toolkit.** Remember the list we made in the improving your energy

section? Things you're grateful for belong on that list, and reviewing it helps to raise your energy.

- **It could be worse.** No matter your situation, there's always someone who has a worse one than you. Don't focus on the "worse", but more on the "At least I have…." and be grateful for that.
- **Write thank you on your checks.** Anxious about the money it takes to get your bills paid? Try being thankful you have the money to write those checks instead. Write "Thank You" on your checks as a blessing for those serving you and as a reminder to yourself to be grateful you can write them.
- **Pick a number.** Find a number of things each day that you are thankful for. Mine's five. A routine puts your head is in a positive space more often.
- **Try to think positively.** Positive energy attracts positive things, so look for what's positive.
- **Post online.** There are lots of negative things online; but regularly posting a few things you're grateful for can not only make your energy more positive, but can also move other people to find gratitude in their lives (and that supports us all.)
- **Find yourself a gratitude buddy.** Just as having a partner for the "Wouldn't it be nice?..." process helped you move your energy up more rapidly and ask for more extravagant things, so can a partner help you with gratitude. He can help you find things to be grateful for when you're feeling down and remind you that things can get better.
- **Have your self an appreciation spree.** Set a timer for ten minutes, and start naming off all of the

things that you're grateful for. Don't just stop at obvious things (a financial windfall, the person you love, your health) but also try including things that you don't necessarily think about everyday but would miss if they were not in your life (literacy, toilet paper, the Magna Charta and all of the rights that we have to this day because of it.)
- **Pray.** If you're on a spiritual path, prayers of thanksgiving are one of the best ways to bring more gratitude into your life.

That's only a few ways to work with the energy of gratitude. If you look at your life, I'm sure you'll find other ways to bring gratitude into your day.

An attitude of gratitude has been found to be an important part of physical and emotional health, and it's a powerful tool for manifestation besides. Whether its prayer, posting or counting your blessings, gratitude helps make your life better.

I think that everyone should have some kind of gratitude practice. I hope that you find yours.

Pulling It All Together

Chapter 25
Pulling It All Together

My husband, Starwolf and I were driving to a party. The rain began to pour down heavily as we approached our destination.

"Wouldn't it be nice if the rain would slack off?" he said.

And suddenly, it dropped to a gentle shower...

I looked at him. He looked at me. One eyebrow apiece shot up and locked in the "isn't that interesting" position.

"Did you see what I saw?" I said.

"Yes, I wished the rain would slack off and it did..." he replied.

" Wouldn't it be nice if the rain would stop until we got inside?" I said.

And the rain stopped. Only to start coming down in torrents after we got in the house (and let me say I'm sorry now to my friends who arrived after us...)

In the end, manifestation is all a question of energy – what kind you have and what you do with it.

You prepare your own energy as much as possible to make it easier to attract things, people and experiences that you'd like. You get clear on what you really want and you ask for it. You focus your energy on that goal and you give more energy to what you want than what you don't want. You do what you can to prepare to receive the good things coming.

You know your own signs of resistance. You watch for them, and when you spot them, you take action to avoid resistance or minimize it as much as you can.

You pay attention when you're doing manifestation.

You revise the process you're doing if you need to, and you take inspired action, using the guidance you've been given.

It all boils down to that basic formula:

Energy + Intention (your goal) + Focus (your process) = Manifestation

Now you know the steps of manifestation and how to put them together; and you have a whole bunch of different tools you can use to do this. At this point, how you use this knowledge is up to you.

We are always manifesting. I'd say that the next question is what are you going to manifest?

Chapter 26
Don't Stop Now…

You've learned how manifestation works. About the nature of energy and how it can bring better or worse things into our lives. How working with your own energy, asking for what you want, and preparing to receive can help you shape the reality around you and attract a better life. You've also learned a lot of different simple ways that you can do this.

We've had a long trip together through the basics of simple manifestation work, but we're coming to the close of this journey.

Don't stop now…

Now it's time to stop reading and start playing with what you've learned. I'd encourage you to play with all of the different types of manifestation work in this book, both to get a working knowledge of all the processes, and to find the ones that suit you best. (Remember, that may involve different ones at different times.)

We are always manifesting – and now that you know more about how that works, you can use that awareness to make a better world for yourself and the people around you.

Here's wishing you fun and joy and prosperity and all of the best things possible coming into your life.

Catherine Kane

Appendix I
Picking a Manifestation Techniques

When picking a technique, you need to think about what fits your unique situation. Things to consider:

I) Do you do this only once (1x) or on an ongoing basis (>1)?
II) Can you do this quickly (Q) or does it require more time (Mt)?
III) Do you think (T), say (S) or do (D) in this technique?
IV) Do you do this alone (A) or with other people (Wo)?
(If more than one symbol in box, you have different options.)

Technique (Chapter Number)	I	II	III	IV
Abundance Beliefs (13)	>1	Q	T	A
"Act as If" (13, 19)	>1	Q/Mt	T/S/D	A/Wo
Affirmations (23)	>1	Mt	S/D	A
Appreciation Spree (24)	1x	Q/Mt	T/S	A/Wo
De-cluttering with Intention (12)	1x/>1	Q/Mt	D	A/Wo
Feng Shui Cures (12)	1x	Q/Mt	D	A/Wo
Gratitude Buddy (24)	1x	Q/Mt	T/S	Wo
Gratitude-Positive Thinking (24)	>1	Q/Mt	T	A
Gratitude-Online (24)	1x	Q/Mt	T/D	A
Gratitude- Prayer (24)	1x	Q/Mt	T/S	A/Wo
Gratitude- Say Thanks (24)	1x	Q	S/D	Wo
Inspired Action (21)	1x	Q/Mt	T/S/D	A/Wo
Listen/Pay Attention (20)	1x	Q/Mt	T	A
My Favorite Things Toolkit (10)	1x	Mt	T	A
Previewing (17)	1x	Q/Mt	T	A
Setting an Intention (16)	1x	Q	T/S	A
Share the Wealth (13)	1x	Q	D	A/Wo
"What if Things Got Better?" (11)	>1	Q	T/S	A
"What if" Buddy (11)	>1	Q/Mt	T/S	Wo
"What if" Group (11)	>1	Q/Mt	T/S	Wo
"Wouldn't It Be Nice?" (15)	1x	Q	T/S	A/Wo

Glossary

"Abundance belief" – Belief that there are enough good things to go around and the main question is how to attract them.

"Act as if" - Method of changing reality by "acting as if" what you want is already achieved, utilizing the resources you already have.

Affirmation - Positive statement repeated to build new beliefs.

Attraction - Using energywork to draw things into your life.

"Catastrophizing" - Mentally leaping to the worst possible conclusion.

Chi or Ki – Terms for energy. Ki (Japanese), Chi (Chinese).

Conscious mind – The part of your thoughts that you're aware of.

Energy - Non-physical element the universe is made of.

Energy field - Personal energy in and around each living thing.

Energywork - Non-physical ways of affecting physical reality.

Ethical - In keeping with accepted ideas of right and wrong.

Feng Shui – Chinese art of arranging buildings, objects and space to achieve energy, harmony and balance. "The way of Wind and Water."

Feng Shui "cures" – In Feng Shui, specific things done to fix problems with energy flow.

Focus – To concentrate attention/energy on.

Free Will - Ability to chose, whether bad choices or good ones.

Gratitude work – Using the energy of appreciation of what's good in your life to attract more positive experiences.

Highest good statement - Part of manifestation request that 1) allows for better results than you've thought of, and 2) ensures good results for everyone concerned.

Incantation – Ritualized words or phrases repeated to produce a magickal effect.

Inspiration - Guidance or influence exerted directly on the mind or soul.

Inspired Action - Action taken in response to inspiration, instinct or hunches.

Intention - A goal or objective.

Invocation – 1) The act of conjuring or summoning with incantations. 2) The act of calling on a Higher Power for assistance.

The Law of Association - Metaphysical principle that says when you have two things with elements in common, what you do to one can affect the other.

The Law of Attraction – Metaphysical principle that "Like attracts like" and "What you put out is what returns to you." Karma.

Lower power manifestation techniques – More subtle methods for manifestation that avoid resistance.

Magick – The art or science of changing reality through energetic means.

Manifestation - Creating something from nothing by non-physical means.

Manifestation process/technique - Method of manifestation.

Manifestation work - 1) The collective methods of manifestation. 2) Engaging in manifestation.

Metaphysics – The art and science of non-ordinary reality.

Mind-body connection - Process by which your thoughts and your body affect each other.

Negative energy – Energy that's more dysfunctional and unpleasant.

Negativity - Giving most of the attention to what's wrong or missing in a situation.

Positive energy – Energy that's more constructive and enjoyable.

Prayers of intercession - Prayers asking the Divine Being to intercede for you or on behalf of someone else.

Previewing - Visualizing a positive result before starting an experience.

Resistance – Beliefs in conflict with what you're trying to achieve that often cause you to sabotage yourself.

"Scarcity beliefs" - Beliefs that resources are limited and not enough for everyone.

Setting an Intention – Choosing a goal to focus energy on.

Spell – Incantational word or formula.

Spiritual Gifts – Skills and talents due to spiritual intervention.

Unconscious mind – Thoughts and beliefs that are hidden but still have an effect on you.

The Universe – General term for the Divine Creator.

Vibration - Energetic speed or frequency of energy, determining what the energy will attract.

Visualization - Mentally picturing an experience; can use any or all of the five senses.

Wishing – Simple folk magick for changing reality.

"Worthiness" - Beliefs about whether one deserves good things or not.

"Wouldn't it be nice" – Manifestation process that avoids resistance by phrasing a goal as a possibility as opposed to a demand.

Index

"Abundance belief" 101, 103-105
"Act as if" 104-105, 137-144
Affirmation 157-162
As specific as you need to be and no more so 24-25
Ask once and detach 65
Attraction 7, 9, 10, 12
Buddy, manifestation 78-79, 87-89, 111, 115-117, 166
"Catastrophizing" 87
Chi or Ki 13
Choosing a manifestation technique 57-62, 177
Cleaning as manifestation 92-100
"Coincidences" 146-148
Conscious mind 9, 12, 16, 18
Energy field 14-18, 27-28, 73-75, 79-82
Ethics 41-56, 109-110
Feng Shui 59, 95-100
Feng Shui "cures" 96
Focus 27-30, 164-167, 171-172
Formula for Manifestation 11, 29-30, 172
Free Will 48
Gratitude work 76-82, 163-168
Group manifestation 88-89
Highest good statement 51-54, 109-110
Inspiration 141-152
Inspired Action 149-154
Intention 21-28, 30, 94, 99, 119-124, 135-136
Invocation 7
The Law of Association 91, 92
The Law of Attraction 7, 16-18, 164-165
Listening to your body 34-35, 144-145

Lower power manifestation techniques 3-4, 31-40
Manifestation process/technique (working with) 57-68
Manifestation Routine 57-59, 63-68, 123-124, 161-162
Metaphysics 119
Mind-body connection 8-9, 122
"My favorite things" toolkit 75-82, 165-166
Negative energy 14-17, 41, 66, 75-76, 83-84
Negativity 31-34, 75, 79-82
Positive energy 14-19, 28, 41, 73-76, 79-81, 83-90, 163-164
Prayers of intercession 7
Previewing 125-130, 138
Qualifier phrase 51-52
Receiving 133-152, 171-172
Resistance 31-40, 59-61, 67-68, 109-114, 117-118, 121-123, 164-165
"Scarcity beliefs" 45-46, 101-104
Setting an Intention 21-26, 119-124
Symptoms of Resistance 35-36, 145, 147, 148
The more the better 65
Unconscious mind 9, 16-17, 32-33, 36, 67, 94-96, 99, 122, 135, 157-158, 160
The Universe 24-25, 28, 102-103, 105-106, 119, 136, 141-142, 145-147, 149
Vibration 13-20, 27-28, 30
Visualization 133-141
"What if Things Got Better?" 83-91
Wishing 3, 7
"Worthiness" 41- 56
"Wouldn't it be nice..?" 111-118, 173

Who is Catherine Kane?

Catherine Kane is a professional psychic, bard, Reiki master, story teller, Christian mystic, teacher, speaker, enthusiastic student of the Universe, maker of very bad puns and overachiever (amongst other things…) Since many of the things she loves doing most, such as teaching, writing and metaphysical work, are about empowering people to find and live their best and brightest dreams, she's come to the conclusion that her Life Mission is to be a Fairy Godmother.

This has led to an understandable fascination with manifestation work.

She has written three other books so far – "Adventures in Palmistry", "The Practical Empath- Surviving and Thriving as a Psychic Empath" and "The Lands That Lie Between" (an urban fantasy novel.) The odds are good that she'll continue to carry on in this fashion.

Visit Catherine at
www.CatherineKaneWrites.wordpress.com
and as Catherine Kane Writes on Facebook

Catherine can also be found with her husband Starwolf as Foresight at
www.ForesightYourPsychic.com,
www.ForesightYourCTPsychic.wordpress.com
or as Foresight on Facebook.

Also by Catherine Kane

Adventures in Palmistry

Your Destiny is in your hands – and you can have a hand in your destiny! Reading palms can empower and enlighten you, giving you the information you need for the adventure of life, and enabling you to help others around you. And it can be a lot of fun, as well. "Adventures in Palmistry" makes palmistry easy and fun. It will put the power of palmistry in your hands.

The Practical Empath- Surviving and Thriving as a Psychic Empath

Do other people say you're too sensitive? Do other people's emotions overwhelm you? Do you carry abdominal weight you can't seem to lose?

You may be a psychic empath, tuned into emotional energy which can empower or drain you. To use that gift to help yourself and others, you need to learn skills that put you in control of your gift.

This is the book to help you do just that…

The Lands That Lie Between- An Urban Fantasy with Morgan and Sam

The day that Morgan lost her job, she knew that change was coming. She broke her lease, threw everything she valued in life, including her cat Sam, in her van, kissed her adoptive family goodbye, and started a cross country trek.

She knew change was coming. She expected that.

What she wasn't expecting was elves, or magick walking in the world around her, or the beauty and the danger of the Lands that Lie Between…

For more information on these books, please visit Foresight Publications at www.ForesightYourPsychic.com

www.ingramcontent.com/pod-product-compliance
Lightning Source LLC
Chambersburg PA
CBHW031954080426
42735CB00007B/393